CAPSIZED

Banshee's Women

CAPSIZED

in the
Coral Sea

by

Jeannine Talley

Published by
Mother Courage Press

Also by Jeannine Talley
Women at the Helm

Library of Congress catalog card number 92-60317
ISBN 0-941300-24-2 (cloth edition)
ISBN 0-941300-23-4 (trade paperback)

Mother Courage Press
1667 Douglas Avenue
Racine, WI 53404-2721

For
Bob Bedford, George Collins,
and Carol Moore.

Acknowledgments

As I begin to write this part of the book, it is exactly one year since we were dismasted. Over the past year hardly a day has passed when I have not realized in a very concrete way that this is not just Joy's and my story but rather, an account involving a very large cast. The overwhelming response to our mishap and our long and expensive task of rebuilding *Banshee* makes a very clear statement that the world has not become a callous, uncaring place. It is the love and concern of so many people that has sustained us when the going was tough.

Quite possibly this book, certainly not in its present form, would never have been written were it not for Federal Sea Safety who organized the search that led to our rescue. This effort involved literally hundreds of persons including the administrative staff at Sea Safety, civilian volunteers as well as Australian Army, Navy and Air Force personnel who flew the aircraft and those who went along as observers. Also pertinent to this effort were the ground crews who worked out the details of the search, everything from amassing available aircraft to deciding the area of the search itself. To the brave and courageous crews on the two Blackhawks who plucked us off the ship, we owe a debt for our very lives.

For Captain Bob Fisher and the crew of the *Maersk Sentosa*, we have nothing but praise for the manner in which they carried out their part of a dangerous rescue. The fact that *Banshee* survived coming up against this ship in rough conditions and that neither of us was injured or killed testifies to the expert skill of those navigating and maneuvering the ship alongside. Not only do we feel gratitude for our lives but also for Captain Fisher's care in seeing that our possessions taken aboard his vessel were returned to us. Among the most valuable of these was our computer and printer, disks containing a book manuscript, my journals covering six years, our ship's log and the charts on which we were navigating when capsized.

We wish to thank Derek Barnard of Penta Comstat for the valuable service he and his wife, Jeanine, perform for cruising

5

yachts and for alerting the authorities to our suspected plight when we did not check in for the 6 a.m. schedule or in a subsequent roll call.

From the time we came ashore, another entirely different cast of people responded to our basic needs, offering food, shelter, clothing and financial assistance. Joy and I have heard the story in America of accident victims being brought to a hospital for treatment and dying on the doorstep because they were not covered by medical insurance. We are most thankful that our experience in Australia at the Rockhampton Base hospital reflects a more enlightened attitude, one committed to providing medical care to everyone. They examined and X-rayed Joy's leg upon arrival, attended to her leg on another day and removed a piece of glass from my foot. For these services we were not charged a penny. We are especially grateful to June Herrington, the Director of Red Cross House, for furnishing the essentials together with her motherly comfort offered in her jovial, buoyant manner.

Much appreciated is the hospitality extended by John and Lorraine Ryan and the concern of Cassandra Winter and Philip who chauffeured us around to various interviews, fed us and gave us cash so I could purchase some reading glasses and essentials, such as toothpaste and shampoo, and arranged for McDonald & East, a major department store, to outfit us each in one new set of clothing.

While many of these people were encountered for just a short period of time, Carol Moore has been our mainstay. To us she has always been available day or night to intervene in any type of emergency. Because of her talent in communicating and organizing, she handled everything from finding housing for us to securing tradesmen to help with repairs. As soon as she learned of our plight, she launched an appeal for us, even going on television to plead our cause. Her energetic action resulted in an avalanche. Help poured in from friends and strangers. As a show of our appreciation, we thank the following people: Allan and Pat on *Smokey Bear*, Eric and Carolyn Van on *Skamokawa*, Bob and Sylvia Wells on *Sylvia*, Les and Sally Jones, Mike and Linda Litner on *Desert Star*, Joanne Livingston and Fritz Warren on

Truly Fair, Janet and Warwick on *Transcender*, Melva and Hilton Ward on *Spindrift,* Nita and John Neave on *Agony*, Tim and Jan Johnston on *Eos*, Lorrie Haight and Harrison Smith on *Akavit*, the Longs on *Eros*, Mike and Ardith on *Sanctuary*, John and Mary on *Counterpoint*, Cliff and Bev on *Mystique*, Ron and Vicki on *Delirium*, Loren and Georgia Murphy on *American Flyer* and Vic Myers. Some donors remained anonymous. To them we also express our thanks.

We feel a special gratitude to Dave and Mary Francis on *Vivant* for coming to Rockhampton to render comfort and much needed assistance. We also wish to thank family and additional friends from afar who sent us love, financial aid and comfort. Among these are my mother, Annetta Shellhouse; Joy's mother, Rena Gamez; my uncle and aunt, Raymond and Nan Culler; Frieda Barna; Libby Burgess; Louise Malone; Jo Register; Janet Myers; Joyce and Jim Irving; Ian and Beth Scarborough and Enid and Bert Emtage.

To the Australian officials, we want to express our thanks for the cooperation of Her Majesty's Customs and Immigration for making our reentry and extended stay in the country for repairs as smooth as possible. We owe a special debt to Dennis Young who met the helicopter and personally arranged to transport Jason, our cat, to Stu and Wendy Penning, who kindly took care of him until we could arrange his return to us in Mooloolaba. For finally seeing that Jason was released from quarantine—after he had served a full nine months—we extend our thanks to John Biggers.

The second miracle to us was the rescue and return of *Banshee*. No one expects to leave a vessel on the high seas and see it again, unless of course one has thousands of dollars to pay salvage fees. Even then, when the vessel is 500 miles offshore, the chances of seeing her again are almost nil, perhaps about as slim as finding two very accomplished seamen who will volunteer to face the rigors of the salvage for absolutely no monetary gain. But Bob Bedford and George Collins are extraordinary human beings, possessing an inordinate amount of compassion. Those two knew, as only sailors can, the pain and agony of losing one's vessel. Bob is also a very determined man who found Mike Carney to donate about 40 percent of the fuel needed to effect the mammoth undertaking. Their gift to us was as precious as life itself. As Joy says, it was like winning a million dollars in lotto. We shall be eternally indebted to these men.

We also give our heartfelt thanks to Bob's parents, Dot and Graham, who opened their home to us during our stay in Townsville. While in Townsville after *Banshee* had been returned to us, we were assisted in numerous ways by others who saw our needs and responded. Our thanks to Jill and Brian Robinson, Ron and Lila Jones on *Pacific Express*, Liz and Lou Miller on *Silver Cloud*, Ann and Bo on *Lionwing*, Brian and Judy Willey on *Banjo* and Kevin and Ailsa McMahon.

Bob Bobbermein will long be remembered for his expertise and care in trucking *Banshee* from Townsville to Mooloolaba. Upon our return to Mooloolaba, we became the house guests of Helen and Peter Turton until more permanent living arrangements were made for us to stay on Jeff Brown's boat until *Banshee* could be made habitable.

Another guardian angel was Keith Lawrie, who generously gave us unlimited free hardstand and launching in his boatyard where we stayed for four months before being ready to relaunch *Banshee*. He was also the first person to contribute to our appeal fund.

More than a few tradesmen assisted in rebuilding the boat, repairing and furnishing parts. Many of these volunteered services or gave us reduced rates and were generous in rendering advice and instruction so we could carry out most of the repairs ourselves. The shipwrights who aided us were Peter Creese, Steve Miller and Ray Seddon. We also thank Nick Wooller for rebuilding most of our deck stainless steel work and for extending, along with his wife Jan, hospitality aboard their vessel on several occasions. Machining of various bits and pieces (and there are hundreds) as well as the designing of our new dodger has been accomplished by Bryon Clissold and his apprentice, Brad Doherty. Clissold has been generous in his time spent with us, reliable and considerate in his prices. Painter Robert Forbes, who had painted *Banshee* just before our departure, kindly resprayed her once her hull repairs had been made at no cost to us for his labor. We also appreciate the helpfulness of Cheryl of Sunshine Coast Marine

Coatings who has supplied many of the materials we needed at a reasonable discount.

Brian Wallace and Dave, the engine mechanic, have been most helpful and cheerful when carrying out engine repairs, often voluntarily doing us a good deed. To brighten several of our days, Brett Tomlinson struggled masterfully to disassemble and reassemble the entire steering system, entertaining us simultaneously with his robust humor. On another occasion, he easily pumped rivets into our new mast to attach the trysail track. Glen DuRietz did a beautiful job designing and making the canvas part of our new dodger.

We greatly appreciate the concern and expertise of Ian Kelshaw who worked hard with us to repair old sails and build two new ones.

For the construction of the new mast, Joy and I worked closely with Greg Gilliam—better known as Grogo—who designed the spar having only the data of our sail plan and the chainplates at his disposal. Assisting Grogo in some of the detail work was Razzle.

Yachtsman Frank Anderson spent two weeks working side by side with us in the initial days of repair and returned three months later to help us launch the boat and work with me on rebuilding the electric windlass. His company was as uplifting as his skills were valuable.

Charlie Miller, the marina manager, has aided in many ways, most notably finding space in the yard for us to store our boom, house our mast while we rig it and our dinghy while we completed it.

Douglas Chippendale, the owner of Dolphin Marine, and his employee David Bates (Batesy) and Carol Moore, a former employee, have all nobly assisted us in finding and ordering parts.

Photo copying of various materials for this book has been meticulously done by Glenda Robson at the marina office. We also greatly appreciate the thousands of other things she has done to make our extended stay in Lawrie's Marina pleasant. Ron, another marina employee, kindly helped us on numerous occasions, operating the forklift so we could easily load things onto *Banshee* while she was resting high off the ground in her cradle.

Joy has put in hours and hours of labor, organizing the work schedule, ordering parts and securing tradesmen for the rebuilding of *Banshee*, and she herself rewired the entire boat. Much of her advanced electrical knowledge was gained from our good friend Ted Perkowski, who generously spent a week designing the new electrical system and continued over the next four or five months acting as Joy's tutor. Ted's wife, Susan, assisted by bringing some parts for us from the States and by doing research there on a suitable VHF radio.

I wish to thank the Bureau of Meteorology Queensland Regional Office in Brisbane for supplying copies of the weather maps reproduced in this book and for discussing with us details of the weather we experienced at sea.

I also wish to express my gratitude to Joyce Irving for reading an earlier version of this book, for catching the typos and offering suggestions that significantly improved the text. I appreciate the sharp eye of Catherine Smith, on board *Salus,* and her keen editorial comments on the final version.

Joy has helped me considerably by remembering details I had forgotten, offering innumerable suggestions for clarifying the text and technical matters, and encouraging me to write this book.

I am especially grateful to my publishers, Barbara Lindquist and Jeanne Arnold of Mother Courage Press, for their concern and assistance and for assuring me just weeks after our dismasting that they wanted to publish my account. I am pleased with the care they have taken in producing this book.

Any errors or omissions are entirely my responsibility.

June 7, 1991
Mooloolaba, Australia

Contents

Introduction

When Joy Smith and I cleared Manly, Australia, on June 1, 1990, bound for Vanuatu, we left when the weather forecast looked most favorable for our passage. Nothing suggested that six days later Joy and I would encounter the worst conditions either of us had ever seen in more than twenty years of sailing. If someone had said we would be overtaken by an out-of-season cyclone, we probably would have dismissed the comment as a joke.

Except for one thing. Both of us experienced some rather unsettling premonitions prior to departure. By far, Joy's were the most persistent and vivid but, not wanting to alarm me and, above all, distrusting the unscientific nature of her intuitions, Joy chose to ignore these feelings. Fortunately I acted upon one of my compulsions—to buy hacksaw blades. Ultimately we probably owe our lives to these blades.

Perhaps the two worst fears lurking in every sailor's mind are either being run down by a ship at sea or meeting the ultimate storm. Some facts about cyclones will indicate just why sailors hold such intense fear of them.

Whether called *hurricane, cyclone* or *typhoon,* it is the same beast, defined on the Beaufort Wind Scale as wind of 64 knots (73 miles per hour) or higher.

From space satellite pictures, hurricanes and cyclones appear as small, flat spirals that seem quite innocuous. Nothing could be further from the truth. When these systems converge on shipping lanes, islands and coastal areas, they wreak great destruction of property, often causing loss of life.

What causes hurricanes? They are the offspring of ocean and atmosphere powered by moist sea air and the heat of condensation. They are driven by the easterly trade winds, the temperate westerlies and their own horrendous energy. Violent winds of lethal velocity circulate around a tranquil eye. Their broad base dominates weather over many square miles, causing the sea to develop a violent surge. Cyclones can extend up to 50,000 feet above the earth's surface.

With a life span of days or weeks, they occasionally attain a velocity of over 200 knots (230 miles per hour). Of all atmospheric disturbances, hurricanes, cyclones and typhoons are the most violent and destructive. Sometimes oceanic waves of more than 50 feet are generated and sometimes the storm surge results in a tidal rise along the coast exceeding 12 feet. No wonder that for centuries seafarers lived in dread of these storms and developed a large body of lore based on numerous signs and weather omens. Many of these observations, such as those based on types of cloud formations and large ocean swells, provide valid indicators, explicable by modern meteorology.

Like migratory birds, cruising sailors schedule their departures and arrivals in the tropical areas of both hemispheres to avoid the recognized season for these super storms. In the northern hemisphere, the hurricane season extends from late May through October, whereas south of the Equator, it lasts from late November through March. The greatest hurricane frequency in the southern hemisphere occurs from January through March.

Ongoing progress in meteorology and oceanography, achieved largely through high-speed computer modeling and weather satellite data, has greatly refined forecasting of typhoons—thus providing ample warning of impending danger. Ocean-going merchant ships and navy vessels have the advantage of speed to outmaneuver such threats, either by avoiding them entirely or at least escaping the worst of such weather.

Although most meteorologists agree to the conditions favorable to the formation of hurricanes and typhoons, there is no universally accepted theory of their formation. Some of the conditions include sea surface temperature of 78.8 degrees F (26 degrees C), below normal pressure in low latitudes (under 1004 millibars or 29.65 inches) and above normal pressure in higher latitudes, a tropical disturbance at the earth's surface moving at a speed of less than 13 knots, easterly winds decreasing in speed with height and extending upward to at least 30,000 feet, and heavy rain or rain showers in the area.

One of the most difficult tasks is forecasting the tracks and speed of hurricane movements. Each track appears to vary, but examination of hundreds of tracks reveals that there are 12 basic patterns they follow.

Like many cruising sailboats, we carry a weather fax on board *Banshee* which enables us to have immediate and reliable weather maps several times each day. Our system consists of a HF radio and a Pakratt, a decoder which interfaces with a laptop computer. If we wish to preserve the weather map, we simply print it, but most of the time viewing it on the computer screen is sufficient for our needs. Unlike large, power-driven ships, sailboats are simply too slow to outrun a massive weather system such as a hurricane. It is ironic. While we had warning of a low heading toward us in our position 450 nautical miles offshore, there was nothing we could do to escape its devastating effects. We departed Australia with a favorable weather pattern in June, a time well past the hurricane season. Yet despite prudence in selecting a time for our passage and the guidelines of our weather maps, we still got caught.

During the six years Joy and I have been sailing the South Pacific, we have encountered storms of 45 to 55 knots on several occasions. While such circumstances are not pleasant, a well found yacht can withstand these conditions—usually far better than the crew. The weather the June storm presented was much worse because once the wind rises above Force 10 (48 to 55 knots), yachts find themselves in survival storm conditions where wind and sea are the masters. Primarily, the severity results from the fact that force exerted by wind does not increase proportionately with velocity but rather with the square foot of the velocity. Doubling the wind velocity results in four times the force. For example, a 52-knot wind exerts a force of 15 pounds per square foot, but 110-knot wind results in a force of 78 pounds per square foot. It takes little imagination to envision what happens to ocean waves in such conditions and it is the sea, not the wind, which poses the greatest danger to vessels.

What we did not know in advance was that this low was an extra-tropical cyclone, a savage winter cyclone. Whereas the tropical cyclone has a warm core, the extra-tropical cyclone has a cold core. Months after we were rescued, Joy talked with the Meteorological Bureau in Brisbane and asked about the weather system we encountered. They confirmed it was a cold-core cyclone. The latter differs from a warm-core cyclone in several ways. Usually the cold core cyclone is preceded by a cold front. It covers a larger area than a tropical cyclone and usually the strongest winds are at the periphery rather than near the center. As we have learned, extra-tropical cyclones are rare. My research disclosed that in July, 1935, this coast was hit by a savage winter cyclone that wrecked the 5,233 ton ship *Maheno* on Fraser Island. Officers on the Japanese ship *Atsuta Maru*, also caught in this cyclone, reported it as the worst weather they had ever encountered off the Queensland coast.

We were not alone in 1990. Several boats were caught in this cyclone and all but one sustained damage of one kind or another. Personally, we have met and talked with several people who were out there and we read accounts of others.

Almost from the beginning, the search conducted by Sea Safety for the *Rockin' Robin* crew was controversial and has been roundly criticized. Since we were also there, we believe we can elucidate some of the problems. We may be able to indicate some procedures and equipment that could be incorporated in future searches to facilitate rescuers in their search and recovery. An analysis of our own situation and responses and an assessment of what happened may provide a kind of checklist for other deep sea sailors and help them to be as well prepared as possible.

I also hope this account acts as a cautionary tale to deep water sailors and would-be long-distance passage makers. Those of us who choose to go to sea must be prepared to take responsibility for ourselves. When you go to sea, you are alone and on your own. No matter how good search-and-rescue teams are, there are times when conditions mitigate against searching and carrying out a rescue operation as well as situations when no one even knows the vessel is in distress. When there in the midst of the survival storm with a disabled vessel and perhaps with physical injuries to the crew, one must be prepared to act independently. Various emergencies and plans for dealing with such contingencies bear thinking about and preparing for in advance. A very important aspect of the preparation is to learn all we can about the experiences of others at sea.

16

Foremost, it is important to try different techniques in handling your boat in different weather conditions. How does she behave when hove to? How does she act when lying ahull? Can she handle herself downwind under windvane or autopilot? Up to what wind velocity can you continue to sail down wind or broad reach without having to tow warps or something astern to slow down the vessel?

It is foolish to assert that in a certain situation one must act thus and so. Too many variables, including the vessel's design, affect how a boat responds to weather conditions. Each person must gain this knowledge personally through experience on his or her own craft.

Years ago when I ran a sailing school called Seaworthy Women, little did I think that one day I would be put to the test. Fortunately, of all the yachts that go to sea, cruising the oceans of the world, few will be capsized, rolled 360 degrees or pitchpoled. It is some consolation to realize these occurrences are rather rare.

Chapter 1

In and Out of Australia

For the past six years, Joy and I have been cruising *Banshee* in the South Pacific. We left Los Angeles at the end of March, 1985, on a voyage that carried us south to Mexico, then westward to the Marquesas, the Society Islands, American and Western Samoa, Tonga, New Zealand, Fiji, New Caledonia, Vanuatu and Australia. We spent a year-and-a-half in New Zealand where Joy taught school and I worked on my book, *Women at the Helm,* which describes our adventures from Los Angeles to New Zealand. We made many friends there and are very fond of that country.

My love of the ocean goes back to my childhood as does my dream to sail around the world in a yacht. I spent the first 22 years of my life in Florida. Although we lived 60 miles from the Gulf of Mexico and about 100 miles from the Atlantic Ocean, I found many occasions to visit the beach. I've always been fascinated by the sense of timelessness the ocean conveys and its power. Yet aside from its might, the ocean imparts tranquility. Watching the surf and listening to it comb the beach fills me with a sense of peace. I've never been actually afraid of the sea, but I have a genuine respect for it. The ocean and the elements are great levelers that know neither class nor wealth. Together they form an impartial judge and jury for those unprepared or foolish enough to underestimate their strength and fury.

Until she was 17, Joy's time was divided between living in the hills of Los Angeles and on a wheat farm in Kansas. She never experienced a hurricane or high winds, except for a Kansas tornado, until she went to sea. From the first time she went on a day sail in her early 20s, she was hooked. She loved the ocean, loved sailing. It became an addiction.

Banshee, a 34-foot fiberglass boat, was designed by Halsey Herreschoff, the fourth generation of a family of famous boat designers from Bristol, Rhode Island. Her beam is ten feet and her draft of 6 feet 7 inches is unexpectedly deep for a boat her length.

She has a fin keel and her rudder design is a spade on a skeg. Although twenty-one years old, *Banshee* is in excellent condition and has proved to be a strong and comfortable cruising boat. Since the yacht was laid up before the oil crisis of 1973, there was no stinting on the resin used in her construction. Probably for this reason she has never suffered from osmosis, the bane of fiberglass boats built from the mid-70s on.

Before I met Joy in 1982, she had owned *Banshee* for twelve years and had sailed her twice across the Pacific—once to New Zealand, once to Tonga—and later to British Columbia and back to Los Angeles. When we decided to go circumnavigating together, I sold my 31-foot wooden Mariner ketch, *Esperanza*, and became part owner of *Banshee*.

Before departing on any ocean passage, we have always carefully checked over *Banshee's* gear and fittings. In general we spend a lot of time maintaining her. Such care and concern has no doubt benefited us innumerable times, assuring us safe and mostly pleasant, usually trouble free passages.

One of the other players in this drama is Jason, our cat. We adopted him when we were in New Zealand and he has been our friend and sailing companion ever since.

Joy is a scientist. She studied and taught biology for many years. She will tell you she is totally left brained and sees things as black and white. Staunchly she pooh poohs ESP, premonitions, out-of-body experiences, spiritualism or anything that can't be unequivocally tested and proven. Consequently one of the strangest aspects of our experience, even several weeks before our departure from Australia, was Joy's growing sense of doom. Even more peculiar was the fact that her premonitions covered not only the disaster, but the rescue of *Banshee*. Neither of us has an explanation for her premonitions, but because they were there before and throughout our ordeal, I will include the occurrence in my account.

For the six months we were in Australia, at least five months were occupied working on *Banshee*. By the time we were ready to set off north to return to Vanuatu, we had painted and varnished the exterior, varnished the interior, replaced our old head with a new one, installed a ProFurl roller furling gear for our genny (something Joy had been longing for for several years), replaced all our ship's batteries and completed any number of other jobs. When we cast off our mooring lines from Lawrie's Marina in Buddina where we had carried out all our work, *Banshee* was gleaming. She looked like a new boat.

The season was moving on. Many cruisers had already left for Vanuatu, New Caledonia or points north along the Queensland coast. We were anxious to get underway, eager to feel the yacht surging over ocean swells and to smell the fresh wind that would blow out the cobwebs collected from our lengthy stay in port. Harbor rot had well and truly set in. One measure of that was the appearance of the yacht's interior. In our five months of easy marina living, the inside had come to resemble a condo more than an ocean-going vessel. It took several days to pack away all the free-floating items which would become airborne missiles under sail.

At long last we took a deep breath. We were ready to leave. We had done a major provisioning, canned our meats, paid our bills and said our farewells. It was time to go to Manly where we would clear customs. On May 21, our friends Mary and Dave Francis from *Vivant* and Ron and Vickie from *Delirium* cast off our lines and wished us bon voyage. The forecast was for 20 to 25 knots southeasterly, not the most pleasant conditions for sailing south to Manley.

After installing the ProFurl, hanking on sails which had been removed for repairs and rerunning the rigging lines, we had not tested anything out. The ProFurl is a roller-furling device that furls the genny to any size, including rolled up completely, and eliminates so much foredeck work that really tires us out on passages requiring many sail changes. Out in the channel we hoisted the main. To our surprise and amazement, everything was led correctly and worked smoothly. We had expected to find some lines braided or misled and were pleased that all was well. Then the big moment came—time to unfurl the genny. Zip. It popped out like magic, just by pulling a single sheet. Gone were the days of removing a sailbag, running jib sheets and hoisting the sail. Now it was permanently hoisted. With the pull of a line we could furl or unfurl the sail to whatever size we needed. It seemed too easy.

It was a lovely, brisk day. The bow plowed through whitecaps as we beat into the 20 knot southeasterly. Three ships bobbed off Point Cartwright awaiting a pilot. With the southeasterly on our nose, we were not making very rapid progress down the coast to Scarborough where we planned to spend the night. Joy was quite concerned about our slow progress, afraid we'd not make our destination before nightfall. Neither of us wanted to be sailing at night in Moreton Bay with its shoal waters, dreadful currents and a terrible chop that develops in southeasterlies.

By noon when we had not even gained Caloundra Heads, we knew it was time to turn back for Mooloolaba. But the time had not been wasted. It had allowed us to do a trial sail and to determine that everything was operative—that is everything except our VHF radio, which was only transmitting intermittently, and our engine. By the time we returned to the marina, the engine was shutting down because of clogs in the fuel line. This problem had plagued us since leaving New Zealand the previous year. Once again we tried to clean the fuel line with a pump, but the gunk simply would not come through the line. Eventually Joy—nicknamed on this occasion "Diesel Lips"—solved the problem by siphoning by mouth. I closely monitored the hose to sound the warning in time for her to remove the hose from her mouth. Out plopped a massive gooey glob. Afterwards the engine sputtered and coughed briefly then settled into a nice, even purr.

Sent off to the technician for testing, the radio proved to have a faulty microphone. We bought a new one.

Three days later when the wind shifted southwest, we made our second departure. At first with only 8 to 10 knots we motorsailed. When the wind came up, I was just about to suggest we shut the engine off when a terrible metallic clang rang out from below. It sounded like the blades of the alternator hitting something. Immediately I cut off the engine. Joy moved the companionway steps and took the cover off the engine to check it out. It was the alternator. A bolt had sheared off. Joy made a temporary fix and we hove to while I helped her reinstall it.

After replacing the alternator, we ran the engine for a short time before the alternator slipped again. It had sheared another bolt. The bracket holding the alternator in place had not been installed properly and was slipping. While Joy was fixing the bracket and installing a second alternator (the bolt had broken off inside the first one and would have to be drilled out), I was sailing the boat until the wind became so light in the lee of Bribie Island we were simply slatting around, hardly moving.

Around 1:30 p.m. we started motoring full speed ahead, wanting to make Scarborough Marina before dark. We just made it. As an animated sunset faded, we pulled up to the Moreton Bay Boat Club dock and made fast our lines. In the pub we paid our fees and arranged for a hot shower. It was a cold night with a biting wind.

The next morning was cold and overcast. I put on three layers and brought out my wool watch cap to warm my head and ears. By 8:30 we were underway, moving nicely downwind on a southwesterly. The surface of the bay was almost flat; we coasted along silently following a course much like a gymkhana, zigging and zagging around sandbars and shoals. We sailed between Mud and St. Helena's Islands, then around Green Island, keeping well off as it shallows a considerable distance out from land.

Once around Green, the sailing was over because our course was right into the wind. We dropped the sails and powered the last three or four miles into Manly Harbour. Momentarily we pulled into a guest dock and checked with the manager at the Royal Queensland Yacht Squadron to see where we could moor. With our cat Jason still in quarantine aboard the boat, we had to moor on some piles. It was freezing cold and the water was filled with brilliant blue jellyfish.

We had just barely tied our mooring lines when two very dear friends, Bob and Sylvia Wells from *Sylvia*, appeared. What a surprise. We had not seen them since New Zealand and didn't know they were in Australia. Their boat was tied only a few hundred yards away. What a lovely reunion we had with time to socialize and catch up on the events of the past two years.

When we first came to Australia six months ago, we had intended to put in at Brisbane. Now we finally succeeded. But, we didn't take *Banshee* up the Brisbane river. We took the train. Up early on Monday morning, we took the 9:37 train from the Lota station into Brisbane. Aside from our desire to see Brisbane, one of the more pressing reasons for going to the city was to fill out our departure forms at Customs. We had learned the Customs procedure well since we came to this country. We told them the day we planned to depart so they could come down to Manly to see us off. Customs was our first order of business; a leisurely lunch at McDonald's on the Brisbane River with a colorful view of the busy waterfront was the second. Then it was off to find a duty-free store that would deliver to the marina, and a quick stop at Boat Books to purchase tide tables covering Vanuatu, the Solomons, Papua New Guinea and Australia.

Early on June 1, a Friday, Customs came, checked us over and left us with our clearance papers. After packing a few remaining things, we were finally ready to put to sea. Bob and Sylvia came over and cast off our lines. Just prior to our departure, a bearded man stopped by and introduced himself as Barry. He and his wife, Margaret, on their boat *Pom Pom* were also planning to set off in a day or two for the Solomons, but, as it turns out, they left the day after we did.

After leaving Manly, our plan had been to anchor overnight at Tangalooma on Moreton Island to avoid sailing against the tide and transiting Northeast Channel at night, but with a fresh southwesterly blowing, Tangalooma was out. It is unprotected from westerlies. Instead we chose to anchor in the lee of Mud Island.

Surprisingly, right in line with the buoys a half a mile off the island, the depth was only six feet. Cautiously I nosed in and suddenly the depth increased to 18 feet, then 20. Now that was more like it. Apparently there was a sandbar surrounding the island, but from the chart you couldn't know that. Sandbars shift constantly in these waters so charts are never accurate. We anchored in 17 feet about one quarter mile offshore. Although the wind continued to howl for most of the night, our anchorage remained flat and peaceful.

That evening I reflected that it had been very difficult for me to break away from land this time. I wasn't quite sure why I was reluctant to leave. I sensed the same thing in Joy, though she didn't mention her reservations to me, and I barely stated mine. One of the last things I did before leaving was to bike into Manly to buy two hacksaw blades. For some reason I had been thinking about buying hacksaw blades for days. It kept coming into my mind, nagging at me. It was almost a compulsive urge. After purchasing them, I bought an ice cream cone and stood in town looking at the traffic, the people milling about and thought—"I'll be at sea and they'll still be here on land." Only later did I learn Joy had the same image, except she felt that the people on land were safe whereas we at sea faced peril.

Once or twice before this I said to Joy that I wasn't ready to leave Australia. It wasn't for any specific reason, just a rather vague feeling that it wasn't time to go. Perhaps, I should have listened to these feelings.

Once our lines were cast off, the feeling receded. It felt so good to be sailing again, to be free. What a beautiful day with wall-to-wall blue sky. We were dead downwind, going wing and wing with full genny and main. With a good high coming on, we might have some strong winds—30 knots or so—for a day, but it should be perfect weather for sailing to Espiritu Santo, Vanuatu.

I had noticed that Joy seemed unduly anxious about leaving. Rushing around to get ready had been stressful. I chalked her nervousness up to our hurried pace of the past few weeks. Later I learned the real nature of her distress. She had a premonition that something terrible was going to happen to us.

We were up at 6 a.m. and underway at 7 on June 2. A strong ebbing tide and a brisk westerly pushed us to the beacons leading into Tangalooma by 8:30. About 15 minutes later we joined the East Channel and proceeded north along the shore of Moreton Island. Eventually this course brought us to the Northeast Channel, a channel no longer used by ships and therefore no longer maintained.

Just before 11 the tide turned and to make sufficient way we cranked up the diesel. By noon we had reached the end of the channel and bore off onto a course of 030 degrees; it was dead downwind. The channel proved exciting, not only because of the strong countercurrent, but because all around, the shoaling waters were often visibly marked by a frothing seaway and lighter colored water.

On a downwind course, we put up the pole for the full genny, a smooth maneuver with the new roller furler. Two highs, back to back, were producing a cloudless blue sky. We knew as we went further north and as the high moved off, the isobars would spread out, giving us lighter winds.

But for now, the weather was so great for sailing, we couldn't help but think of the contrast between today's weather and that of our first landing in Australia.

* * * * * *

Australians are renowned for their shortening of words. Whether this trait springs from an inherent laziness or from an abiding sense of humor is a subject that would probably make a good psychological study. I suspect both factors play a part, perhaps helped along by a frontier mentality that shunned things too proper.

The term "Oz" for "Australia" is of recent coinage. In the 1970s, liberal thinking university students, disillusioned by the extremely conservative bent of their country—especially its materialistic and militaristic leanings—began ironically referring to Australia as Oz. The cognomen has stuck, perhaps because the irony has been lost on those who would most vehemently reject it. Our voyages to and from Oz seem to have many affinities with Dorothy's journey to the Land of Oz.

As readers of the *Wizard of Oz* know, Dorothy's transport to Oz occurred under weird circumstances, caught up as she was and swept away by a fierce tornado. We too got caught up in horrendous and unexpected weather the first time we arrived here. To press the parallel one point further, Dorothy had her dog, we had our cat, Jason. And to add to that, Joy spent some of her growing up years in Kansas!

On the fourth day out from the Chesterfield Reefs in November of 1989 on our way to Australia, we began having portentous weather. Up until that point, we had such light winds that we either carried our largest sail, a drifter, along with full main, or we ran the engine.

Completely in keeping with the mild weather we'd been having, the night of November 20 was calm and summery. I took the watch from 8 p.m. to midnight. It was glassy calm, a starry night. Jason sat beside me in the cockpit because it was cooler than below in the cabin. The engine was purring along, as it had been since just before sunset. To allow some cool air to circulate below, we had all three hatches wide open in addition to all ports except for two defective ones that we had boarded up before departure from Vanuatu. We still had the full mainsail up for stability, but it was sheeted amidships because there was no wind to fill it.

At midnight, Joy took over the watch. Jason stayed on deck with her and for the next two hours the same conditions prevailed. Then around 0200, Joy suddenly felt a cold wind strike her out of the southeast. Within about five minutes, it was blowing 20 knots and started raining. Below, the cold, whistling wind woke me immediately. I jumped up and both of us were moving as fast as we could, closing hatches and ports. Even before we had everything secured, the rain had become a drenching downpour. The wind was steadily rising and within half an hour it had risen to 30 knots.

Once the hatches and ports were secured, we began to reef the main because we were being overpowered with just that single sail. It was remarkable how rapidly the seas came up. The change was so abrupt it was as if we had passed an invisible partition separating one ocean from another, one night from another.

Forty-five minutes had elapsed altogether by the time we reefed the main. Now the wind was up to 45 knots and gusting higher! Quickly we threw in the third reef. Until sunrise it continued to blow 45 to 50 knots. The seas continued to build. When the sky lightened at dawn, the ocean and sky seemed to flow together, so alike were they in color. The wind dropped to 35 to 40 and we added the reefed staysail to have enough sail to punch through the large seas.

On the morning radio net we learned that a very high pressure system had hit the Brisbane coast, sending the barometer up five millibars overnight. At 0200 our barometer registered 1009 and by 0900 it was up to 1012. Throughout the day the wind held at about 30 knots, the barometer rose yet another millibar and the sky continued gray but developed more definition with streaks and cumulus cloud.

About an hour before sunset, I saw a ship whose bearing didn't change. We were almost certainly on a collision course. The radar confirmed that the ship was a little over eight miles away, closing and definitely on a collision course. Joy called them on channel 16 but there was no response. After repeated calls, always conveying the information that we were a 34-foot yacht limited in our ability to maneuver, relaying our course and position and that we appeared to be on a collision course with them, there was finally an unintelligible, abrupt grunt and then complete silence. When they were as near as a mile and a half, still heading for us, we decided it was time to alter course. On the radio we announced what our new course was. Silence. Total silence. By now it was nearing darkness, but even as we sailed across the ship's wake, she still showed no navigation lights even though it was past nautical twilight. Long after they steamed away, I still saw no light from her. She was like a phantom ship, oblivious to our presence. But for the two of us who saw her and the radar which confirmed it, I would have thought I was imagining things.

Shortly after the ship had gone, the wind began to increase. Joy, who seems to have an uncanny ability to feel these things before they happen, insisted that we drop the mainsail entirely. We barely had it tied on the boom before the wind was roaring 45 to 50 knots. By now the seas were 20 feet plus. In these conditions we usually stay below, looking out every 15 minutes by standing on the companionway steps and sliding the hatch back just enough to poke our heads out and look around. With breaking seas, we have to keep the hatch boards in. Even opening the hatch to look out runs the risk of taking water below. In such conditions—large seas and a pitch black night—it is almost impossible to see anything. Because of the size of the seas, it is very easy to miss a ship, even one close by. The perfect solution, of course, would be to operate the radar. Unfortunately we simply don't have enough battery power to run the radar constantly. When conditions are this rough, we can't run the engine for charging so we have to be conservative in our use of electricity. Carrying running lights is a priority at night and often to conserve energy we turn the refrigerator off. The next thing to go is the satnav, but the running lights stay on so that other vessels can see us.

About midnight Joy sighted another ship. This was especially bad news because we still had 45 to 50 knots and were only reaching under the reefed staysail. In heavy winds and mountainous seas, dodging a ship would be difficult. Fortunately the ship responded to our call, but they didn't see us. We didn't even make a blip on their radar! We were learning fast that you have to look out for yourself out here. Usually ships don't see you. Terrifying but true.

What we did then was turn on our radar and tell them what our bearing was from them. They still could not see us and they were only three miles off and yes, on a collision course! We then turned on our flashing strobe light (these are illegal, incidentally) and they saw it. Now they could see we were on a collision course. They wanted to know what course we were steering and then said they would steer around us, keeping off three miles. It was so nice to find a ship that was keeping watch and kind enough to take evasive action. We thanked them for their consideration and wished them a good night.

Rough conditions, lack of sleep and insufficient food were taking their toll—I was becoming seasick and unable to keep any liquid down. I was in a tailspin—unable to eat, loss of desire to do anything but lie in my bunk and sleep, along with depression and inability to concentrate. I could force myself to do what I absolutely had to do on deck and with great agony stand my watches, but I wasn't operating at optimum. Fortunately Joy was not seasick, but she was very tired, near exhaustion, yet feeling that she should do more than her share because she knew I was not well. But I insisted she rest and let me take regular watches.

By daylight the wind decreased again to 35 to 40. We went outside and raised the triple reefed main to help us plow through the colossal seas. The sun, bright and intense, bounced off the seas. Once outside, I began to feel better immediately. *Banshee* was flying over mounds of deep blue water, slowing and slewing when breaking seas cascaded over her decks. The minimum height was about 15 feet, most were seas were closer to 25 feet. Not infrequently they were spilling over us, hissing and growling as they hurdled past.

I was searching the horizon for Lady Elliot Island, a small low piece of land that we expected to see off our starboard. I saw nothing. Joy turned on the radar and it picked up the island, only five miles off and dead ahead! Obviously we were making more leeway that we thought. We fell off. As we learned only hours later, we could have saved ourselves much time and effort if we had hardened up and kept Lady Elliot to our starboard. We did not do that because the chart showed a shoal area and we were uncertain if it would be dangerous in these conditions.

It was a fast, rough sail coming around Lady Elliot. Once on its west side we hardened up as much as possible, but we still were unable to point to Bundaberg which lay directly into the eye of the wind.

When darkness came, Bundaberg was still 20 miles distant. We had no desire to tackle the entrance to the river at night. Since both of us were absolutely exhausted, Joy suggested we heave to for the night, expecting that we would hold our position or not lose too much ground. At first it was rather smooth being hove to. At least it gave us a chance to have a decent hot meal, but within an hour the wind picked up to 40 knots and we were thrashing around wildly.

Heaving to was a big mistake. The powerful wind and current were rapidly pushing us onshore. Joy woke me to say we had to put up sail and move out or within two hours we would be on the beach.

For several hours we tried to sail just under the reefed staysail, but this small sail area gave us too little drive through the short, steep chop. We were hardly any better off than we had been hove to, perhaps only staying in place! At 5 a.m. we hoisted the triple reefed main. Still the wind was out of the wrong direction for us. We'd be tacking our way to Bundaberg and so far it didn't seem the wind was going to moderate. When we tacked we could hold a course of about 210°, but the course to Bundaberg was 150°.

Suddenly we noticed *Banshee* was moving more slowly. The wind had dropped and we needed more sail. Now I could see the coastline and with the added sail, we were once again moving. The sad thing was that the ground we lost while hove to for four hours took us 12 hours to regain.

Joy had been below talking on the ham radio for some time. Afterwards she decided to plot a fix from the satnav. Very alarmed, she came topside and told me we were actually being pushed backwards and in the same position as five hours earlier! Therefore we would never make Bundaberg. She wanted to turn around and run to Gladstone, feeling we could make that port before dark. I replied that something was wrong with the satnav fix because I could tell by watching the shoreline that we were in fact advancing. I could see that the satnav fix was way off.

By now the wind had dropped even more and I convinced Joy we really needed to have all our sail up—genny and full main. Of course the seas were still big, so it was a smashing sail, but we started to move and that made my spirits improve tremendously. Finally another satnav fix came in and it was correct. What apparently happened was that Joy had been transmitting on the radio for some time and it affected the log which electronically informs the satnav of our speed. Because the batteries were low, the transmitting caused a drain that made a drop in voltage and the computer (satnav) did not like that situation.

We had been asked to alert Bundaberg Air and Sea Rescue (BASR) that we were on our way and advise them of our ETA. They asked us to keep them posted as to our progress and even told us they could offer assistance if we should need it. We were rather surprised when, with our second contact, they said they had been concerned about us as they expected us to contact them much earlier. We had talked to them about 24 hours previously, but told them until we got closer we would be in contact with a ham net who was following our progress. Only later—about a week later—did we learn that someone on a vessel we did not even know called BASR and told them *Banshee* was in trouble! Also, as we learned later, word was out that *Banshee* had come to grief. No doubt this misinformation had a lot to do with the 24 hour period when there was no contact with BASR. Additionally, the conditions were severe, bad enough that two local trawlers that set out turned back to port. One never made it and ended up on the rocks.

For the first time in several days, we were under full canvas, our decks awash, making five to six knots, tacking from east to south. It was glorious weather with almost cloudless azure skies. Even though we stayed five to ten miles offshore, the water was very shallow, only seven to eight fathoms, indicated by its light blue-green color. Many groups of dolphins crossed our bow throughout the day. Except for an occasional lone mountain, the shoreline was flat and featureless.

Nightfall found us about 18 miles off the entrance to Burnett River (about the same distance off as the previous evening when we hove to) but having to tack meant we were still many hours away. BASR said they would talk us into the entrance when the time came, and if necessary, someone would stay past ten p.m. to monitor our arrival. That was extremely kind and made us feel good. The entire Coast Guard of Australia is comprised of volunteers. They work very hard and provide a valuable service to people off their coast.

It was a spectacular sunset. The sky displayed just about every shape of cloud from horizontal bands to puffy light cumulus. There was no stinting of color either, orange, rose, mauve, yellow, red glowing over the gentle bulging blue-gray hills. It was the kind of sunset that lasts and lasts, the colors and tints modifying slowly, becoming more brilliant one minute then taking on an entirely different tone. I didn't want to blink as I might miss some delicate shift.

Suddenly the last glow faded. Deep blackness enveloped us and then, it was as if the friendly earth had dropped away and we had embarked on the seas of some distant planet. The wind rose and whined menacingly through the rigging. *Banshee* slammed over on her side, as if hit by some gigantic hand, and the seas bounded over the rail with an agitated hissing.

"What's happened?" Joy's voice betrayed her dread and bone-weariness.

"The wind's come up, howling."

She was below putting away the dinner dishes and I was sitting outside keeping an eye on everything. We agreed, with great reluctance, that we needed to reef again. Reefed, *Banshee* drove more smoothly through the water, but no doubt about it, we were racing along and the seas were becoming more disturbed—just when we thought everything was calming down.

About every two hours Joy called BASR, giving them an update of our position and conditions. We had also asked them to give us the light characteristics of the lighthouse and its longitude and latitude. They wanted to talk us in and reiterated that someone would be there as long as we needed it—all night if necessary. That was reassuring because we had no chart of the entrance or the Burnett River. We were using a sea chart loaned to us by George Emtage and it was about 30 years old. Of course the natural features had not changed, but the lights and other navigational aids had.

Finally BASR could see our running lights from their raised position inside the harbor. They had plotted our last satnav fix (as had we) and confirmed that we could tack, and sailing 180 degrees magnetic, point to the lighthouse and sail on in on that tack. Just after we tacked, the wind started screaming again and we decided we needed to drop the genny and put up the staysail. We relayed this information to BASR, telling them we had to go back on our easterly tack to do the reefing.

No sooner had we gone on this tack than the wind dropped again, so we resumed our previous course still carrying the genny. When we were no more than four miles off, on our final approach, the wind began to blow harder. We didn't want to enter the river with this much sail up, mostly because we didn't really know what to expect. We tacked again and this time dropped the genny. Neither of us liked what was happening at this point. The staysail was on the deck with the reef still tied in and we knew taking out the reef and running the sheets for this sail would take a lot of time as well as energy. The time factor, however, was really the critical thing. There was a strong current and it would knock us down so badly we would lose a lot of ground and have to spend several hours making it up. At this rate we might not get in until daylight. We were determined not to spend another night at sea.

To make matters worse, when Joy went forward to drop the sail, she discovered that the diesel fuel jugs, tied to the lifelines, had come loose and were jammed under the overturned dinghy on top of the staysail. The jugs had to be resecured and that was also

33

time-consuming, especially as the boat was rolling fiercely under just the reefed main.

I was trying to hand steer, to keep us as close to the wind as possible, difficult without more sail up and the windvane wouldn't handle it under these conditions. I dreaded losing ground while we made sail changes. Suddenly it occurred to me that perhaps we could motorsail with just the main. Joy concurred. So, once again we headed back onto our southerly course, aiming for the lighthouse.

Now we were talking continuously with BASR. They plotted each new bit of information we got. I kept having the feeling, though, even after they said we were on a good course, that we were too low and would end up on the enormous sandbank jutting out for some miles to seaward. Finally Joy turned on the radar and it showed an obstruction off our starboard about four miles off! She reported this to BASR and also told them that for the first time our depth sounder had just read four fathoms. They could see us and they couldn't imagine what the obstruction was, but they were concerned about the four fathoms. We weren't about to continue on this course and they agreed that we had to turn east once more.

We did. By now it was almost midnight. We were frustrated and very weary. Twice BASR had asked if we would like them to come out and guide us in. Each time we had refused, but now, we decided with the latest development, if they offered again, we would accept their assistance. They offered and we accepted. About 45 minutes later they came alongside and told us to follow them.

Once we were inside the leads, I was glad we had an escort. Both of us think of leads as a range, one light lined up above another which you steer to. We weren't prepared for what we encountered. The leads were a lane, a channel marked with red lights on the port and green lights on the starboard. These proceeded for several miles up the river. Joy had to be my eyes because standing at the wheel with the dodger flap down, I couldn't see as it reflected ambient light and I dared not stand up on the cockpit seats to see because there was so much surge and current tugging us this way and that. Our main was still up and, going downwind, it created a lot of pressure along with the surge, making steering tricky. In our present situation it was impossible to drop the sail because we were downwind.

After a wild ride part way up the river, the guys led us to a turning basin where we could drop the sail and get ourselves ready to anchor. Of course after our hours of conversation on the radio, they were just as curious to see us as we were them. All of the guys had come—three of them—on the *Bundy Rum* to escort us in. They were jovial and quite pleasant, exchanging small talk with us and joking. It took us a while to sort out the chain. In all the boisterous sailing, the chain had rolled over and over on itself and had to be straightened out before we could anchor. They then took us back down the river a short distance and we anchored in a rolly swell. It was almost 3 a.m. when we collapsed into our seaberths for a short five-hour snooze.

Such was our arrival in Oz.

We had yet to be introduced to another of Oz's wonders—Customs.

At 8 a.m. we were up having breakfast and by 8:30 BASR called to say Customs was on the way. The agent would go up the river with us to Bundaberg to clear in, if that was agreeable with us. It was.

Fergus, the Customs officer, was an alert, teasing 26-year-old who joined us. Two hours up the river took us past fields of sugarcane and barren flat land with a few scattered trees, mostly gums. The river curved and twisted, sometimes running deep, sometimes shallow. Once we scraped bottom with a soft thud. Finally we were coming to the port town of Bundaberg. Yachts were moored along the shore and trawlers were tied up on the opposite shore. Fergus directed us to the town wharf and there we tied to our friends Janet and Warwick on *Transcender*. Having heard us on the radio earlier in the morning, they had come by to say hello before coming up the river. We had not seen them since Tonga, three years before.

Fergus had finished filling out our papers when we arrived, so he left. Very soon after our arrival the next official boarded, the agriculture quarantine inspector. We had just finished paperwork with him and handed over the few fresh foods we had when the animal quarantine officer appeared. I was answering his questions, but was somewhat distracted when I realized the former man had suddenly just started tearing apart our boat, confiscating this and that which he was dumping into a huge black plastic garbage bag. Joy was giving me helpless looks of despair, and Bob, the official I was dealing with, also seemed to have a rather pained expression. I had a very strong feeling that our boat was being invaded. I saw the man dump container after container of our dry stores into the bag—many kinds of beans, whole wheat and then jar after jar of our bottled meat. (I couldn't help thinking of all the hours I had spent preparing these jars.) In went eight jars of chicken, turkey, and pork and pounds of dried beans and peas.

Later we learned that he even took tinned foods which were not banned. Once the ordeal was over, we both realized that had we not been so exhausted we would have requested permission to bond the items he confiscated. Not having had much sleep for the previous three days, neither of us was thinking too clearly.

We were somewhat vexed and perplexed the next day when a boat came alongside with the animal inspector and another man in uniform. Why were they coming out? I'm afraid Joy's voice was almost hostile as they approached. Nonetheless we asked them aboard. Bob introduced Dennis Young to us, saying he was the animal quarantine officer from Gladstone.

Both men came below and there was an uneasiness as they sat down. We were really feeling invaded, especially after Bob had even returned the previous day to tell us what arrangements we could make for Jason when we hauled out. Australian regulations stipulate that an animal entering the country from a foreign source must be quarantined for nine months. He would not be allowed to stay on the boat when we hauled out unless he was caged and then Bob would have to come twice a day to feed Jason— for which we would have to pay an exorbitant amount. Another option was to bond Jason to a foreign vessel, but not an Australian one. Still a third option was to put the cat down. Bob had taken Jason's picture with a Polaroid and I half expected him to say they had to have a paw print too. Now I noticed that Dennis Young had come aboard with a Polaroid. Did he have to have a picture too? It was getting to be a little much. (Fergus had warned us about the bureaucracy!) Jason was sleeping quietly on the settee and didn't even blink an eye when they came in and sat down. To my absolute amazement one of them said, "Ah, he's very domesticated, isn't he?" What did they think we had, a tiger from Borneo? There was still that uncomfortableness, as if they didn't know how to begin to say what it was they came out for. Finally, Bob seemed to relax a bit and started to speak what was on his mind.

"I was very embarrassed yesterday with the way the agricultural inspector handled things. In fact I was having trouble filling out my papers. He really wasn't very nice."

"We were upset too," I replied. "If we hadn't been so tired, I'm sure one of us would have asked him what he thought he was doing. We should have been given the option to bond our food, shouldn't we? After all, we have a bonding locker."

"Yes, I think you should have had that option. What do you think, Dennis?"

"Yes, of course. That would be reasonable."

Joy had a few things to get off her chest. "You know, he was pushing me aside, being very rude. And he went through the cupboards and lockers just pushing things aside and knocking them around. Several times he said, 'I don't know if this is banned or not, but to be on the safe side, I'll take it.' He really didn't seem to know his business and his manner was most authoritarian."

"Yes, I noticed that," Bob said with something of a hurt expression on his face.

"That's most unfortunate," Dennis said. "Perhaps you should register a complaint. What do you think, Bob?"

"Yes, I think they should. I'll also write a letter, stating what I saw of his behavior."

We set up a meeting two days hence when we should come to Bob's office with the letter.

Bundaberg, fondly called Bundy by the locals, possesses the atmosphere of a small town of the American West. Situated to one side of the railroad tracks, it is a linear town, running a mile or so along the tracks, but only three blocks deep. The buildings, mostly two stories high, have remodelled facades of a nondescript style on the ground level while the upper stories retain the old decorative turns and scrolls from 19th Century architecture. On the ground level, these unpretentious structures house restaurants, take-out foods, shoe stores, variety stores, pharmacies, ice cream parlors, stationeries, clothing stores and banks. The post office and library, late 19th Century vintage, are sedate, imposing structures. There is nothing really British about the town, nor does it resemble New Zealand. More than anything, it looks and feels American.

Bundy makes its living on sugar cane, rum, truck farming and fishing. It is rural but even so the town has its share of visitors, judging by the number of hotels. There are four sizeable hotels right in downtown Bundy. Sizeable means only two stories high, but in keeping with the town's linear concept, stretched out for the length of a block or half a block. The first floor level is divided between the reception area with the remainder given over to a restaurant and pub with package store and ice vending.

Or are the hotels just an excuse to have a pub? One doesn't have to be in Australia long before realizing the Australians take their drinking seriously, especially the men, especially their BEER. Certainly not all, but a fair number of Australian men adhere to the tough frontier type, not entirely unlike the American Wild West cowboy in their demeanor. In their dress, however, they would never be mistaken for an American cowhand. All wear a type of felt or leather hat that resembles that of a Texan, but has slightly different variations. For example, Queenslander's hats are likely to have a flattened crown and a medium-wide brim that tips down in front and back. In summer Aussie cowboys shed Levis and cowboy boots for shorts and thongs—or as one cultured Australian phrased it, they "dress in their stubbies and thongs." Stubbies is a double entendre in Australian as it refers to short bottles of beer and to very short shorts, worn by men, not women.

Anyone coming to Australia should get one thing straight from the start, Australia is a man's country—like the Marlboro ads. Here a man has his mates with whom he's apt to feel more comfortable than with women. Women have their place, their uses—cooking, cleaning, childbearing, the occasional roll in the hay—but otherwise they tend to be a kind of impediment best ignored. A mate, after all, is not your wife, but a male friend. In fact male bonding seems every bit as developed as in a primitive society where men and women lead separate lives except for sexual encounters.

One of the results of the American Revolution in 1775 was to cause England to send convicts to Australia. Before the revolution, England had sent about 1,000 convicts a year to Maryland and Virginia. With British prisons crowded to overflowing, decommissioned ships were turned into prison ships. With the ships riddled with disease and sinking on their moorings, it was soon realized something had to be done to alleviate the dire misery. King George III agreed that prisoners could be transported to the area of Botany Bay. What is called the First Fleet, 11 ships with 1,486 persons arrived in New South Wales on January 18, 1788 to begin settlement of Australia. About half of this number were convicts.

For the next 80 years, 157,000 convicts were sent—three times as many as had been sent to America. The first years were equally difficult for all, characterized by scarcity of food, failed crops, death of many sheep, cold weather, wrecked supply ships from England and difficult relations with the Aborigines. In England, Botany Bay gained such a terrible reputation that convicts would choose death rather than "transportation" to Australia. By 1819 still about half of the population in Australia were convicts.

Nearly a century later on January 1, 1901, the Commonwealth of Australia was born. Only gradually has the country worked toward becoming a fully independent nation. The adopted form of government is modeled after British and American systems. Each of the six states elects 10 senators for a six-year term, and the House membership is based on population. But the prime minister, if defeated on a vote of confidence, must call for new elections in the House. Unlike American voters who are apt to be lax about exercising their right to vote, Australians must vote or pay a fine.

Not only is Australia the "Down Under" continent, some of its ways are a bit topsyturvy. For example, the liberal party is called Labour, the principal conservative party is the Liberal party and the National party—the ultra-conservatives—usually forms a conservative coalition with the Liberals.

We entered Australia in Queensland (pronounced with equal stress on each syllable) and stayed in this state for six months.

Located in the tropical region of Australia, Queensland resembles nothing so much as a mixture of Hawaii with wide sand beaches, rolling surf, bright green islands, fields of sugar cane and pineapple, palm trees, Florida and southern California.

We found ourselves ecstatic to be back on land after our arduous voyage. One of the first things was to feast on favorite foods and indulge in a big ice cream cone. Very quickly we learned one of the local epicurean delights is prawns—tiny ones, middle-sized ones and banana prawns (giants). Directly across from where we moored was the fishing fleet, coming in daily, delivering their fresh catch.

About the second day when we were motoring up the river in *Nessie,* our hard dingy, we spotted *Shalmar.* Naturally we went right up to say hello to Wendy and Stu Penning, but there was no one aboard and it appeared they were gone for a while. We later inquired about them and learned they would be returning in about a week. The surprise was seeing them here because when we parted in New Caledonia, they were bound for Fiji and other points east, intending to be gone for a whole year.

Things were just beginning to die down from our encounter with the agriculture quarantine officer when to our immense astonishment another dramatic thing happened. We stopped at Customs to see Fergus because we had to file our cruising plan. As soon as Fergus saw us, he broke into an impish smile and said, "I heard about your rescue on the radio this morning." His eyes had a devious twinkle.

"Rescue?" We both asked incredulously, "What rescue?"

"Oh, what they said on the radio, that Bundy Air and Sea Rescue went out and rescued *Banshee.*"

"Rescue! We weren't rescued, you know that Fergus," Joy said indignantly. "What radio station?"

"I know you weren't rescued. I'm just telling you what I heard on the radio. The local station." He was laughing at Joy's response.

We filled out our cruising papers, designating all the places we intended to go and learned the procedure we were to follow while in Australia. Every time we came into a new port, if there was no local Customs authority, we had to mail a postcard—furnished by

Customs—to Customs. If there was a local agent, we had to phone him within two days of arrival. At least foreign yachts no longer had to attach a nasty large red sticker with on "F" on each side of the bow that removes the paint when you remove it! About two years previously we'd heard about the dreaded red "F." (Without much effort anyone can guess what yachtie humor did with the "F"!) It was a short-lived practice because visiting yachts raised a tremendous hue and cry that even made the intrepid Australian Customs back down.

After leaving the Customs office, Joy and I talked about what Fergus had said about the rescue, but we concluded he was just teasing us. We forgot about it until lunch time when we went into a Chinese restaurant. The waitress came up and exchanged some pleasant remarks. Every time she came to the table with something, we engaged in more short conversation and she had learned we came to Australia on a yacht. Just as we were about to pay our bill and leave she said, "Are you by chance the two *girls* they rescued?"

"What!" Joy almost shouted. "What do you mean?" (For once she was so concerned about the rescue she ignored the reference to "girls"—one of her pet peeves.)

"I read it in the paper, was it you?"

"God, no! And did you hear it on the radio too?"

"Yes, I did."

"What paper, what day?"

"Oh, I'm not sure which day . . . Let's see. About two days ago, I think."

"Do you have the paper?"

"No, but the office for the local paper is just two doors down. They'll have a copy." She paused and then continued. "Was the article about you two?"

"I guess so." Joy sighed. "We weren't rescued. We were escorted in by the *Bundy Rum*. There's a big difference between being rescued and being escorted."

"Yes, there certainly is," agreed the lady amiably. "Well, go see the paper. Talk to them about it."

"We sure will," Joy said emphatically. "We sure will. They are going to print a correction. We weren't rescued!"

The poor lady behind the newspaper desk must have thought a cyclone came through the door. Joy was still worked up and muttering disclaimers rather loudly. She asked the lady for a copy of the paper with the article, and the clerk pointed to a stack on the end of the counter.

We went through several issues before we found it. It said we had been "lost" and "disoriented" and the *Bundy Rum* "rescued" us. It was just too much for Joy. She stalked right up to the lady behind the counter and said, (surprising me) "Rescued my ass! We weren't rescued! Where did they get that? Rescued my ass!" Joy was furious but comical at the same time and the lady was handling it well and laughing.

"If you don't agree with the article, go upstairs and speak to someone in the editorial office."

We found the stairway and soon were speaking to a young woman who patiently listened to the whole story. It seems some PR person had phoned the paper with the information for the notice. She assured us that the paper would not take the liberty of changing the wording—so it must have been reported to them as a rescue. She said she would write up and print our response and it should be out in a day or two. It was out the following day.

Was this foreshadowing of our ultimate return to Australia six months later?

A few days after Wendy and Stu had come back, they drove us down to Burnett Heads in their car so we could thank the folks at BASR for their help and inquire about why we had been reported as being rescued. Working that day were Clem and Jean. Jean said she was also amazed at the notice in the paper because it did not reflect the report which she had given to the PR person. Then Jean showed us what was in their log and the information given to PR for the paper. Public relations had changed "assisted" into "rescued!" At least now we knew who was responsible. Some people like to make headlines for the paper. Maybe they thought a good story about a rescue would bring in more donations. In Joy's opinion the PR person said it was a rescue because we were two women. I guess we'll never really know the reason. The Australian Coast Guard is run by volunteers and supports itself by donations.

We donated to this worthy group and commended them for their able help and assistance.

On the appointed day, we went to keep our appointment with Bob, the animal quarantine officer. We had our letter of complaint in hand as well as a list of the confiscated foods and the replacement cost in Australian dollars. This list was not just an estimate dreamed up out of our heads. We had done our homework by going to various grocery stores and pricing each item. The total came to only $50 and some odd cents. Obviously, money was not the issue.

Bob would not be able to see us, the secretary said, as he was out on a job. However, Dennis Young would see us when he got in from Gladstone in about half an hour. He was right on time and escorted us into an office. After a few pleasantries I handed him the letter which was typewritten and the list which was handwritten.

Very much surprised he said, "Ah, I see you have a typewriter on board."

"No," Joy piped up, "a computer/word processor."

"Oh, well, I didn't expect that on a boat."

He read through the letter, commenting to me, "You certainly know the English language and how to use words effectively."

"I'm a writer," I smiled.

"I see. Humm . . . Yes, well, recently our department crossed horns with another writer, and the whole incident created big news in the local paper. Caused quite a stir."

I didn't know if he was fishing to see what my response would be, hoping perhaps to dissuade me from pursuing such an explosive course—if I had such an intention—or if he was simply being friendly. He photocopied the letter and list and handed me the copies, assuring me that the letter would be forwarded on to the appropriate official in Brisbane. We thanked him and left.

That was at the end of November. By mid-February when we had not heard anything, Joy decided to call. She finally got to the right chap. He began by saying there wasn't anything they could do. After all, it was just our word against the agent involved, who had denied that his behavior was anything less than exemplary. Joy reminded him that Bob had witnessed the entire scene and said he would write a letter to substantiate what we said. The agent then said he would get back to Joy after contacting Bob.

A couple more weeks went by with no word and then one day a letter came and with it a check for exactly the amount we had specified. That action, even if it did take some prodding, did a lot to first establish my faith in Australia and Australians.

During the first week in Bundy, we were putting ourselves and *Banshee* back together so we could begin our journey south to Brisbane. After talking to Peter on *Wild Spirit*, moored at the Royal Queensland Yacht Squadron in Manly, we decided to go there and called to make reservations for the pile moorings, knowing that with the cat we weren't allowed to take a slip.

About two days before we were to leave, Stu and Wendy stopped by for a visit. We mentioned to Stu that we needed to replace our ship's batteries. They were five years old and not holding a charge. Stu convinced us that we should replace them in Bundaberg where he thought we could get a better price, and he volunteered to drive us around to look for batteries and also to lift them in and out. The confined areas where they go are more physically demanding than Joy or I can handle. They are very heavy 105 amp, deep-cycle batteries.

What a big job. Hundreds of wires (so it seems) had to be disconnected and reconnected. Because the new batteries were slightly smaller, we had to build shelves and make cables to tie them down. It was an incredibly tedious job that took almost a week to complete. Meanwhile the entire boat was torn apart and without electricity we couldn't cook on the propane stove unless we disconnected the solenoid, which we didn't want to do. That left us with a one-burner primus that we'd never used. Breakfasts and lunches were no problem, but dinners for two nights when we had no electricity were impossible. I took food to *Shalmar* and cooked for all of us in their galley.

Mornings we placed the primus in the cockpit and fired it up. What a smelly affair. It sputtered and coughed and flared up several times before finally burning and then took forever to boil water.

Our one concession to things electric was the refrigerator. We kept it hooked up to one battery powered by the solar panels and the wind generator because the small freezer was full of meat we had just provisioned with in preparation for our departure.

I'm glad Joy understood the wiring. To me it was a mass of red, green, black and purple wires crisscrossing and crammed together in a meaningless jumble. She made a diagram and labeled the wires and, having initially installed everything before we took off from Los Angeles, she understood the system. Who would have dreamed then that she would be completely rewiring the boat once again in a few months? When the job was done, we had new batteries, ready for another five years—sort of. We didn't know then that one was defective and would have to be replaced when we got to Lawrie's Marina at Buddina.

During this time we were living in utter chaos, stumbling over gear stacked inside and heaped up in the cockpit. Working on a boat as you live on it is sheer madness. Many times it means putting things away at night to have room to prepare meals and sleep, only to pull them out again the next morning.

Finally on December 10 we left our mooring on the Burnett River at about 4:30 p.m. and went to the fuel dock for diesel and water. It was blowing like stink as we pushed down river against tide and wind. We passed flat land fringed with mangroves, gum trees and acres and acres of sugar cane fields. Here and there water from irrigation systems streaked across the sky, fanned out into mist by the blustery wind.

The forecast was for southeast winds going northeast. We would not even consider trying to go to Fraser Island in a strong southeasterly, as we'd be banging right into it in the famous short chop of Hervey Bay. We had already sampled that on our way into Bundaberg. It took about two hours to get to the sugar loading wharfs where we anchored next to some moored yachts. This was only about five miles from the river entrance.

At 5 a.m. we were up but not ready to leave until 7. Discouragingly the wind was still southeast—as it had been all night—but it was light. As we powered down toward the mouth, the swell increased and the wind strengthened, making us question if this would be a good time to cross the bay. At last we could see where we had come that black night when we followed the *Bundy Rum* through the leads.

Two weeks later on our way down the coast, we encountered yet another of Oz's wild tornados.

On December 23 we were sailing for Pelican. Only thirty minutes after getting underway, the tachometer stopped. This meant the batteries weren't getting any charging. This kind of failure had first happened to us in New Caledonia where Joy had had to replace the cable from the alternator. We had to replace it again in Bundy. Had this gone again? After so short a time? There was nothing to do but keep going for Pelican and check it out once we anchored. We anchored at Pelican at 5:30. Not only were there many trawlers anchored there, waiting, there were six or eight sailboats and, as we watched, one crossed the bar under sail. It was a little boat too.

Joy removed the engine cover to discover it was not the cable, but a broken wire from the alternator plug. Although we had no spare plug, she thought she could jury rig something. It was a delicate job which proceeded by trial and error. In the meantime, someone arrived in a dinghy and yelled hello. Going on deck, I was surprised to see a large jovial fellow, the one we had watched sail in over the bar! In a heavy Dutch accent he said he was Herman. He invited us over for some fresh prawns, pointing with a stout arm over to his boat which was rafted up to a larger boat. I thanked him for his invitation and explained we would come as soon as the repair was done, about half an hour we thought.

Half an hour turned into an hour and then longer. Joy was having problems finding a connector that would fit. Finally she discovered that one side of the plug was smaller than the other side. About this time Herman powered up in his boat with his girl friend. He yelled out that he had come to pick us up. By coincidence Joy had just completed her repair. We quickly scurried around, grabbed a couple of bottles of wine and jumped into our dinghy so he could tow us up wind to his friend's boat, *Whisper L*. Soon we were shaking hands with Jeff and Mary Terese, the owners of a beautifully maintained Lyle Hess-designed boat.

From a large bucket of prawns sitting in the cockpit, we eagerly drew them out and pulled away the shells as we gorged on them. Joy and I thought this was dinner, but soon Mary Terese

46

disappeared into the galley and began whipping up something that smelled delicious. It was a mouth-watering prawn curry dinner consumed amidst good conversation and much boisterous laughter. Before we went back to retire for the night, Jeff assured us that going over the bar in the right kind of weather was a piece of cake. They were departing early in the morning and we could follow them if we liked. They were heading for the same place as we, Mooloolaba.

Up at first light, we found an overcast day, still and almost windless—exactly the right weather for crossing the bar. The trawlers had left during the night in search of prawns. So much for the advice to follow the trawlers out, unless we wished to exit the bar at night. There was activity aboard other boats, including *Whisper L.*

As we were hauling up our anchor, they too were raising theirs. Soon we were side by side exchanging greetings. We paused to let them go ahead of us. The pass and the sea beyond were dotted with returning trawlers. Several times we altered course slightly to avoid an incoming trawler with its nets flung out like the wings of a giant insect.

Actually our anticipation of the bar had built up to the point that crossing it was anticlimactic. Jeff was right, in this weather it *was* a piece of cake. We simply kept the range markers lined up astern for several miles until a second set of range markers lined up, at which time we changed course accordingly. *Whisper L,* moving at a snail's pace because of her small engine, required us to drop into neutral periodically so as not to overtake her. The further to seaward we progressed the more swell we encountered and the shallower it became as we neared the bar. Because of *Whisper L's* ambling speed, the transit of Wide Bay Bar seemed agonizingly slow. Once clear, a breeze stirred. We hoisted the genny to assist the main, but it soon became apparent that the wind had not really settled in. We had to drop the sail and proceed under power once more.

Now as earlier, the engine vibrated rather badly, especially at low RPMs. Upon starting out, it had made a terrible racket and Joy had inspected the engine but found nothing amiss. We kept the revs up high enough to avoid the vibration. At last, about midmorning, the wind gradually filled in out of the north just as we had anticipated. Up went the genny again and off went the engine. Roughly staying about five miles offshore through the day, we could see occasional buildings at scattered settlements along the coast. Within about 10 miles of Mooloolaba, we began seeing isolated highrise monoliths that towered over a desolate landscape.

By now the wind was starting to howl, throwing whitecaps at our beam. All day we had been towing the fishing line with numerous false alarms when it would zing and stretch out momentarily only to go slack again. Having seen a plethora of massive jellyfish, we suspected they were tangling with the line which rapidly pulled right through them. Suddenly the line really stretched taut as an overtuned guitar string. We had a big one! Everything was happening simultaneously. The wind was screaming—making us heel excessively—and overcanvased as we were, Mildred, our name for the wind vane, was steering an inexact course. I disconnected her and started hand steering. I wanted to help Joy with the fish, but if I took my hands off the wheel for a second, we would fly up into the wind and the sails would madly flog. Joy was fighting the fish, reeling in then stopping, working it in order to tire it out. Finally she had it alongside, a very large spottie mackerel. With one swoop she swung it over the lifelines, but instead of the fish landing on the cockpit floor, it somehow came to rest on top of the dodger. Joy frantically tugged on it to pull it into the cockpit, but unexpectedly the fish careened into her arm, its teeth cutting a large gash just above her elbow. Not even realizing she had been injured, Joy managed to toss the fish to the floor. Suddenly there was blood everywhere. The thrashing fish was flinging it all over the cockpit and Joy's blood was bubbling out and dripping. Not being eager to be immersed in a bloodbath, I jumped up, each foot astride the cockpit, hoping to escape. From this precarious purchase, I was fighting to steer the overcanvased boat.

Even though blood was spurting from her arm, Joy knew she had to drop the genny immediately before conditions got totally out of hand. She grabbed a dirty old rag and momentarily pressed it to her arm to stop the bleeding. Then she tied it tightly so it would exert pressure while she went on the foredeck to drop the genny.

Once things were under control, Joy cleaned and bandaged her arm. Yet another problem confronted us. For a good hour, perhaps longer, we had watched with concern as the sky in front of us grew darker and darker. Some strange-shaped, threatening black clouds congealed into more ominous masses while long, jagged lightning flashed across the amassing cloudbank. Soon prolonged and muffled thunder rumbled, echoed and rolled in palpable sound waves. All too rapidly the horrendous mass was closing in on us. At first it seemed it was merely a thunderstorm that would pass in front of us. Now, by the minute, it was rushing head long towards us like a stampeding bull. What had been distant was now breathing down our necks. Lightning speared the water all around and thunder boomed with earsplitting loudness.

At 6 p.m., the Mooloolaba lighthouse loomed only about six miles away. Previous to the storm, we had been concerned about arriving before dark, which seemed marginally possible. But now a more pressing concern was: could we make the breakwater before the storm overtook us? Minute by minute this hope was evaporating.

We thought we could see *Whisper L* some miles to our stern. Before leaving Wide Bay Bar, we had agreed on a VHF channel to monitor. We had not spoken to them for several hours, so Joy decided to call them. Much to our surprise, they had just heard a weather report that said the storm we were seeing was out of Brisbane. It had hit there with winds of 50 to 70 knots! It should be less severe for us and last only about an hour.

By now the menace was almost sitting on us. The wind had picked up. The sea was tumultuous. Clearly we would not make the harbor before the storm broke. To be safe we needed to alter course and go out to sea where we'd be clear of hazards. To do that, we needed to raise a headsail so we could beat our way offshore. First we needed to reef the main and hank on the storm jib in preparation for the worst.

It was a race between us and the storm. While Joy was hanking on the storm jib, I watched the tempest closing in. Now the lightning was striking all around us. Its jagged neonlike spears knifed into the sea as thunder clapped almost simultaneously. The storm had us in its grip. I didn't like steering in these conditions, with my hands on the stainless steel wheel, one bit. Electrocution seemed too imminent. We needed to get below where we would have some shelter, a modicum of protection from the lightning, and we needed to disconnect our antennas to prevent blowing up all our electronics in case we got hit.

The sky had taken on a very weird appearance. One area held an emerging egg-shaped mass ten shades darker gray than the surrounding sky. What fascinated me was the smooth almost satin texture of this dark egg which hovered right on the sea. Directly behind us the sky was sooty, menacing, mean. Surely this angry monster would devour anything it swept over. What was in it—high roaring winds, horrific rains? I wondered and shuddered.

Just as the first big drops of rain hit, Joy had the storm jib hanked on. Quickly we hoisted the tiny piece of 12-ounce sail and sheeted it home. Next we set Mildred steering and raced below to disconnect the antennas. The wind had risen to about 30 knots, but with our shortened sail we were riding it out easily, even making about two knots to seaward.

Suddenly a devastating rainstorm struck, totally wiping out the shoreline and lighthouse from view. Nothing was visible past our bow. Heavy rain flattened the sea, the wind died. With the loss of wind we were simply bobbing up and down, a cork being carried at the will of the current, and the direction of drift was towards shore, towards danger. We had almost no margin of safety between us and the shore, five miles at most. We had to move out to sea, quickly. Joy went outside and took the wheel. Before she even got there she was drenched. We got the engine on. When she said she was cold, I grabbed my rain jacket and pulled off my shorts. I went out to relieve Joy so she could come below and dry off and put on her foul weather suit. Now we were powering offshore.

Over the next hour the wind was up and down. Accordingly we had the engine off and on. Slowly but surely we were working our way out to sea. Finally with the fireworks over, we plugged in the electronics. Once the depth sounder showed 14 fathoms, we began to breath more easily. Still the rains continued to come and go, by turns heavy and light, only gradually tapering off, but through the grayness nothing ashore was visible, not even the Mooloolaba light. One thing for sure, it was not over yet and we were well into the second hour. We both knew it was just a matter of time before heavy winds would howl.

What a way to spend Christmas Eve, riding out a storm at sea! What we really wanted now, craved now, was a snug, cozy harbor where we could be warm and relaxed enjoying a nice dinner, an eggnog, a little Christmas cheer.

But that was not to be. Dinner for us was a bit of chocolate, a muesli bar and a glass of water. At one point the wind had become so light that we went on deck to shake out one reef. Just minutes later, however, the second part of the cyclonic system was upon us. We started to shorten sail again, but before the third reef was tied in, I could feel it in my bones and hear the dreadful roar of a crescendoing whine.

"Don't bother with the reef," I shouted to Joy. "Let's just drop the entire sail."

Just in the nick of time, too. A full 50 to 60 knots slammed us over and heaped the sea into a swirling mass of breaking foam and wayward streaks. It was howling, moaning, shrieking. Joy retreated below to notify the Coast Guard of our position and to get a prognosis of how long this dastardly mess would continue. I stayed on deck to keep watch for ships. Some of the boisterous seas washed into the cockpit and up the leg of my foul weather pants. It felt very warm in contrast to the air and wind.

It was a good hour before I saw any lights and then, disconcertingly, I wasn't at all sure what I was seeing. Perhaps a ship, but if so they were not responding on channel 16. Then the light just disappeared. About 15 minutes later I spotted a flashing light off our port stern, bearing due south, and determined it was the Mooloolaba light. Our course had shifted with the wind as it went from east to northeast to north and as we carried on, northwest.

Around 11:30 p.m. we worked out a plan for the night. The wind had decreased as the monstrous front had passed. Presently the wind was holding at 35 to 40 knots but would continue to drop. We could reach northward and then jibe and sail south again, waiting for dawn when we could head for Mooloolaba.

Through the early morning hours, the wind decreased steadily to about 15 knots. We alternated watches, changing about every hour and a half. About 2 a.m., realizing that we just could not clean the fish because both of us were very tired, we had to throw it overboard.

At last Joy woke me, saying it was almost sunrise. I got up and we jibed the boat around onto a course of 210 degrees magnetic, pointing toward where I had seen the barest glimmer of the Mooloolaba light. Heavy mist or rain blocked out the entire shoreline. As we were sipping a cup of coffee, the sun burst over the horizon. I didn't like the looks of the blanket of reddish-orange sky to the east. It fitted the folk rhyme, "Red sky in the morning, sailors take warning."

After the brilliant sunrise, it began raining lightly and the Mooloolaba light disappeared entirely except for an occasional pale loom appearing when the light flashed. By now the wind was pretty light, but until we were only about five miles off Mooloolaba light we continued to sail. As we closed land, the mist thickened and the light vanished. Joy turned on the radar and we started the engine. Bang, clang, it vibrated and made a horrible noise. We shuddered and wondered what was wrong. I raised the revs and it sounded more normal. I hoped the engine would make it, because we really needed it now, especially with such poor visibility. Additionally, we didn't know what to expect at the entrance to the harbor, which can be tricky in certain conditions as it is very shallow. Therefore it is mandatory to follow the channel markers. I was just hoping we would be able to see and not be fogged in (or should I say out?).

The Mooloolaba light sits atop Point Cartwright. As is true of most points along this coast, shallow water extends off the point a good distance to seaward. In this case it is about two miles. Between the radar and the depth sounder we were able to keep nosing our way in toward the breakwater. Finally hazy, murky shapes started to materialize as we crept in cautiously. The string of isolated highrise buildings stood on the shoreline draped in gray wetness. Immediately to our port was the opening in the breakwater, just as the radar had been indicating when we could see nothing ahead of us but opaque pearl gray. A bar straddles the entrance and both of us subconsciously sucked in our breath and held it until we had cleared without bumping bottom.

We had been told that we could tie up to a floating dock intended for visiting yachts to use until they find a slip or a pile mooring. The guest pontoon was just inside where the channel started to broaden. There were several rows of pile moorings, all occupied by trawlers. At first we passed the floating dock, not recognizing it, but seeing nothing else that looked likely, we turned back with our lines ready to tie up.

I missed on my first try. The approach was easy enough but I miscalculated how strong the current was and slowed too soon with the result that we simply drifted away from the dock quite rapidly. But the second try was perfect and it was a simple matter to secure two lines. Here we were—Christmas morning at 8:30 in Mooloolaba—starved and weary. We had told Mooloolaba Coast Guard that we were in, tied up to the floating dock, and we asked if we might have permission to remain there until the following day as we just wanted to eat and sleep. Later we called them again to relay that until someone came to fix our loose motor mount, we would not be able to move the boat. One of the first things Joy had done after coming in was check to see what the problem with the engine was and she discovered the front motor mount was loose. In fact the nut securing the mount had fallen off. We ate some breakfast, slept for a couple of hours, then enjoyed a very large Christmas dinner midafternoon finished off by plum pudding with rum and whipped cream. Then we crashed again and slept for hours.

For the whole week after arriving at Mooloolaba, the big news on the radio was the damage caused by the freak tornado that hit Brisbane and kept us at sea on Christmas Eve. The damage in the Brisbane area totalled a cool $10 million dollars, with the suburb of Redcliffe receiving the brunt of the destruction. The nearby Coast Guard wind gauge registered 100 knots before it and other equipment was ripped off the roof! The met bureau classified the storm as a class two tornado.

The day after Christmas was Boxing Day, celebrated by all British descendants, I think, except Americans. We had strong doubts that we would be able to get a mechanic, called "engineer" in this country, out on Boxing Day to check our motor mount. However, Joy contacted the Coast Guard again with our request. They replied and then someone else from Lawrie's Marina came on the radio saying he thought he could find an engineer for us. He promised to call back in a couple of hours. Two hours later he called, saying he would bring the engineer right then, if it was convenient. Yes, by all means bring him, we responded.

It was blowing pretty hard even in the harbor. Keith Lawrie brought Brian in his Avon dinghy, and they had quite a boisterous, wet ride against the wind. I stayed outside and chatted with Keith while Brian and Joy checked the engine. Brian tightened the mount, checked it for tolerance and also checked the aft mounts, but he found they were fine and the alignment of the engine was okay. However, he recommended getting a new mount in the next few weeks because he thought it was stripped out. He was afraid to tighten down very hard, so in time it could vibrate loose again.

In the meantime I had been speaking with Keith about a pile mooring at his marina and he said he had one we could go on. We were planning to stay just one night before heading south to Manly and Brisbane. Keith and Brian came with us and we towed Keith's dinghy. We passed the Mooloolaba Yacht Club and marina and a little further on we turned down a narrow canal. It was lined on both sides with palatial homes with docks in front. Tied up to them were sailboats, luxury power boats and even some trawlers. We could have been in Newport Beach, California. It was near low tide so I asked Keith if it would be deep enough for us. When I told him our draft, he said no problem in the canal, but we'd never be able to go on the pile moorings. He would put us in a slip. We said we couldn't do that because Jason was in quarantine. Keith explained it was not problem, he would put us in a double slip so we could tie away from the slip, being about six feet from the dock on all sides. He said another American yacht had done this several years ago and animal quarantine had no problem with it.

Keith put us in a double slip for the price of one, quoting us a daily rate, a weekly one, and a monthly one. Obviously we could stay longer than a day, if we chose. Amazingly after all the hardship and strain, we had landed in the lap of luxury. Imagine, we had running water and electricity dockside and on shore hot and cold showers and washing machines and driers! How soft, how plush. But it also meant it would make painting and varnishing so much easier (and we had planned to paint the decks and varnish).

How amazing when events occur as if they had a mind of their own. Somehow these happenstance things always pan out far better than if we had struggled for months to coordinate arrivals, departures, trying to anticipate each calamity and be ever prepared.

And so it was on Boxing Day, unbeknownst to us, this small difficulty with the engine was to be a decisive factor that would determine the next few months, changing all our previous plans. To pervert an old cliche, we fell into the dung heap and came up fragrant as honeysuckle.

We felt we had arrived at the Emerald City of Oz.

We decided to stay for a month before moving on, hoping to have all our work on the boat completed by then. It was more expensive than we would have liked, but we would not need to run our engine every day to charge up our batteries, so we would save on fuel and engine wear. What we didn't know was that one month would stretch to two and then more to include the entire season in Australia. The list of things to do on the boat grew to include so many unexpected repairs and replacements that we ended up with no time to do any more cruising or sightseeing. We stayed at Lawrie's Marina, working, working, working.

* * * * * *

And now here we were leaving Oz for Vanuatu and it was June 3, 1990.

During the night the wind steadily dropped. By sunrise it was so light we ran the engine for one and a half hours until the wind began to fill in somewhat. Beautiful cloud formations circled the sky at sunrise and the temperature felt much warmer than the previous day. In 24 hours *Banshee* had gone 95.6 miles. Now, we were making about three knots with the westerly behind. Rather than sail the rhumb line, we wanted to make as much easting as possible early on, knowing that further north there's a good chance the trades will tend more easterly. A low far south of us, generating a strong southerly swell, was going to wallop New Zealand, but it would not send anything our way. Such a lovely, peaceful sail. Jason slept in the cockpit during the day, lulled by the easy motion.

Joy busied herself with several repairs. She strengthened the alternator bracket and replaced the alternator battery cable (this was the third time it had died in a year). She replaced the solenoid wire to the key switch and rewired the auxiliary fuel pump wire.

During the night of June 3, the trade winds picked up to 25 knots and squalls sometimes went to 40 knots. The new furling jib certainly made sailing much easier. Instead of dropping the sail as the wind picked up and hoisting a smaller sail, we simply rolled in the genny to whatever size was right. It almost seemed like cheating! Just before Joy went to bed, we reefed the main. With the reef in, we still scooted along at six to seven knots. Heavy winds made up for all the light stuff of the previous day. Squalls continued through the night, one after the other. Each was of short duration, but often quite fierce. Before night was over, we furled the jib down to nothing but a small slip of sail. By morning the wind dropped to 15 knots. The squalls were finished, but they left the sea very confused and irregular.

At 9 a.m., June 4, the wind picked up again and shifted almost due east. Now it was difficult to make easting. On this passage, as on others, we checked in with Tony's Net, a radio network that keeps track of yachts at sea, in the morning and the Pacific Maritime Net in the late afternoon, giving each net our position, course, speed and weather conditions, including barometric pressure.

Just before sunset on the evening of June 4, the wind increased. We shortened both sails and by morning the wind was blowing a steady 25 to 30 knots out of the ESE. Now about 30 to 40 miles east of Cato Reef, our course was just a shade east of north. We hadn't had a good satnav fix for several hours. The sun was shining, but breaking seas made it too wet to sit outside. We stayed below reading and listening to music.

Chapter 2

Capsized and Dismasted in the Coral Sea

At noon on June 5 when Joy brought up the weather map on the computer, she let out a loud shriek.

"Look at this!" she exclaimed, followed by a profusion of seafaring profanity. "We need to print this map. There's a damn low of 1008 that's formed off Cape York Peninsula! It's not moving now, which just means it's going to deepen."

Joy's face and voice conveyed her serious concern. Our barometer read 1020 and was falling. The forecast from the radio said heavy swells with large seas. Winds to 35 knots. No one we talked to on the radio seemed very concerned about the low, but Joy was unusually disturbed; I thought almost irrationally so.

Momentarily the low was stationary and deepening—which is exactly what lows do when immobilized. The high that was pushing us along was blocking the low. It was just a matter of time before the low would begin moving. Chances were it would move south following the Australian coastline.

Through the day the weather steadily deteriorated. By midmorning we had a triple-reefed main and a half-rolled genny, but by afternoon, with increased winds and building seas, we furled the genny, dropped the main and went to a reefed staysail only.

Twenty-four hours later, on June 6, we replaced the reefed staysail with a storm jib set on the staysail stay. This maneuver was quite difficult because of heavy, confused seas with heavy, gusting winds. In order to drop the reefed staysail, we had to backwind the sail and then wrap the downhaul; we have one attached to every sail, around a cockpit winch so it could be winched down. Once we had hoisted the storm jib, no easy feat in these condition with breaking seas crashing over the deck and the boat rolling wildly with no sail to steady her, we had to jibe back onto our course. With only one sail up in these seas, the boat would not tack. Jibing was extremely tricky since we had no way on and were just pivoting in place while standing still. It was evident to me that if we caught a breaking sea the wrong way, we could easily be broached, pooped or even flipped over. Waiting until the right moment, I held my breath and then spun the wheel hard over. Slowly we started to turn. I watched a wave which seemed to be rushing to smash into our stern. My heart pounded and then, as tons of white water raced forcefully onto us, *Banshee's* stern gracefully lifted as the sea broke and howled under our keel. I could have hugged *Banshee*. She was proving her worth and would continue to do so.

By now the wind was 45 to 50 knots, accompanied by torrential rains and unusually rough seas. The low had dropped to 1000 millibars and was moving toward us at a speed of 15 knots.

Joy became more and more agitated and concerned. I tried to reassure her, but nothing dissipated her anxiety. When she decided to join Penta Comstat's roll call, I knew she was very concerned. We were already on two radio Network roll calls, why another? She responded that if something happened to us, Penta Comstat was in Australia and they could notify Search and Rescue immediately, whereas the Pacific Net wouldn't do anything for several days and Tony's Net would probably be even slower to respond.

As we later learned, Joy's apprehensions were well founded. Dr. Roger Badham, weather forecaster for the Olympics, America's Cup and other yacht races, described the weather pattern we experienced as a big high pressure system moving through the Bight and by Monday, June 4, it caused strong southerly winds. By June 6, the high was situated in the southern Tasman causing compressed isobars that created a strong air flow. Also by June 6, a weak tropical low was developing further north in the Willis Island area. The low began to move rapidly into the Coral Sea at a rate of approximately 300 miles a day. It was therefore going to cross our path and we would be trapped between the two weather systems before finally being overtaken by the low. By June 7, the isobars were very close together. It is not the intensity of the low that is so bad, according to Dr. Badham, but the intensity of the pressure gradient between the two systems.

With this weather coming our way, what strategy should we adopt? There were three possibilities. We could heave to but we ultimately rejected this option for two reasons. The wind was mostly easterly. Kenn Reefs lay about 30 miles to leeward. Heaving to meant we could be pushed down onto the reef. Another problem with this option was that with little or no sail up, *Banshee* would occasionally present her beam to the seas and could easily be rolled onto her beam ends. Our past experience with heaving to in breaking seas seemed to place the boat in a vulnerable position, in effect, making us a sitting duck. In heavy seas, especially sharp, steep, irregular seas, *Banshee* responds better with some sail up so she is lively, not dead in the water.

A second option was to run with the wind and sea. If we chose that, we would need to slow *Banshee* down or we would be in danger of pitchpoling—turning ass over teakettle. Also, we felt it would be chancy expecting the Aries windvane to steer us in these conditions either downwind or on a broad reach. Previous experience had proved that heavy, confused seas were difficult, if not impossible, for the windvane to handle on these points of sail. Still a third concern was that if we turned southwest, we might be putting ourselves into the very path of the low, perhaps substantially increasing our actual time of exposure to the awful storm that in the end packed hurricane force winds. We had no way of knowing then, but eventually the low veered to the east, coming directly over us!

The third possibility—the one we selected—was to continue on our course going north. This course put us on a close reach with the seas about 50 degrees off our bow.

Even having made our decision, Joy continued to be very agitated and pessimistic. Now she told me about her premonition that something horrible was going to happen to us. I argued that we had been through terrifying storms before. "Not this bad," she retorted, "and it's going to get worse."

We were not the only yacht in this area battling mountainous seas and intense winds. On Penta Comstat's roll call, we heard *Pom Pom* report in, whose skipper we had just briefly met before leaving Manly. *Pom Pom* was about 30 miles north of us. They had cleared the reef and he intended to heave to until conditions moderated. There were other boats out here that we would only learn about later.

Around 8 p.m. Joy called Penta Comstat and talked to Derek Barnard. For all intents and purposes, this was a Pan call (pending emergency) though she didn't label it as such. She told Derek conditions were extremely bad and she arranged a radio schedule with him for 6 a.m. on June 7. Joy's next words chilled my blood. "If we don't come up at 6 in the morning, it will be because we have a serious problem." I could hardly believe my ears. This concerned me because I knew Joy was expecting the worst. Why was she so certain?

Later we learned that Derek sent a telex to Sea Safety that very evening with a copy to Townsville Radio and Brisbane Radio advising them of the situation—just in case.

After talking with Derek, Joy contacted Brisbane Radio with a similar message as to conditions and our position. She turned off the radio, but left it tuned to Brisbane Radio's frequency.

As the night progressed, conditions deteriorated even more. Our normal speed under storm jib only was about 2.5 to 3 knots, but in squalls the speed jumped to an alarming 4.5 or in excess of 5 knots. I say *alarming* because our increased speed was an objective indicator of how much wind velocity had increased. I watched the knot meter anxiously when our speed accelerated and felt myself relax a bit when the speed dropped after a squall had passed. All too frequently, seas broke over us with a frightening crash that made me think it was miraculous the boat could withstand such tremendous forces. Each time one of these pounded us, all three of us jumped. But it was not just breaking seas. More alarming were the times when we dropped with a shudder into a trough. I suppose we were dropping 15, maybe 20 feet. I really didn't want to think about it. Much as I tried not to let it, Joy's apprehension was affecting me. Always *Banshee* has been a dry boat, but in these unusually heavy seas, seawater poured through the fastened ports and hatches when a big sea broke over us. I wondered many times if *Banshee's* hull was being stressed too much. Would a port give way or a hatch be snatched off? Everything forward in the v-berth was absolutely drenched! This had never happened before.

Not long after speaking with Penta Comstat, Joy removed the foam pad from her bunk and placed it on the cabin sole (floor). She's never done this before, but I knew why she was doing it. She was afraid we'd be rolled. Sometime before I met Joy, she had been sailing in the Southern Ocean from New Zealand to Tahiti when *Banshee* was knocked down. Joy was thrown from the high side into the overhead, breaking her back in two places. This was her fear. I knew. I said nothing and she said nothing. Later she told me this is when she resigned herself to our fate. We were going to be in distress, but she felt there was a light at the end of the tunnel. Somehow we would come out of it alive. Once resigned, Joy went to sleep immediately. Even the noise and motion as we were tossed and dropped didn't wake her.

Keeping watch in these conditions was impossible. It was too dangerous to open the hatch, especially in the squalls. No point in trying to look out; visibility was almost zero because of the heavy rain and spume. We turned on the strobe light at the masthead as it can be seen at greater distance than our tricolor masthead light.

Jason was curled up with me on the low berth in the main saloon about 18 inches above Joy, asleep on the floor. Sometimes I dozed uneasily until breaking seas and the motion of the boat falling into troughs kept waking me, each time renewing my dread.

Suddenly I heard the hissing, deadening roar of a wave rushing down upon us. I shuddered and waited. I sensed it was coming for us. With a thunderous crash it smashed us over 30 or 40 degrees and, before *Banshee* could right herself, another growler hissed and roared down upon us unleashing its awesome fury. It must be a rogue wave, I thought, perhaps two of them in succession! Two gigantic waves towering over the others. The second one struck with a decimating explosion. It knocked us down. The impact was like being thrown against a concrete wall. I felt myself rising up to the overhead and then coming back down onto my berth. Simultaneously there was the deafening sound of shattering glass and cans flying across the boat—and the cracking of the mast. I remember thinking: so this is what it's like to be capsized. During the knockdown, everything seemed to slow down. I was not aware of being flung violently, rather it was as if

I drifted down to the ceiling and then once again down to my bunk as *Banshee* righted herself.

I don't know how many degrees we went over. I can only guess that it must have been somewhere between 135 to 140 degrees. This estimate is based on our hull shape which gives us a high range of stability. The greater the range of stability, the quicker the boat rights. We went down and back up in less than a minute.

I smelled kerosene and only realized later when we turned the light on that the trawler lamp had dumped its contents on me while the glass chimney sprayed millions of glass bits over me. Yet, I was not cut!

Joy was asleep when we were capsized. She woke and spoke in a rather calm voice, considering the circumstances. "It's gone! The stick is gone!"

"How do you know?"

"I hear it—that thumping is the mast pounding against the hull. I knew this was going to happen. I've had this terrible premonition for days." The emotion had returned to her voice, betraying alarm, concern.

She got up. Upon moving, Joy experienced horrendous pain in her left leg where a rapidly swelling lump had risen just under her knee. She thought it might be broken. I noticed a broad red streak running down her leg. She must have crashed against the table as we rolled. She maneuvered her leg carefully as she climbed the companionway steps, cautiously cracked the hatch and looked out on deck, "The mast is down. The dodger's gone too! We must think about what to take in the raft with us."

"The raft?" I asked, stunned at her suggestion. "First we'd better find out what's happened, what kind of damage we have." My mind was in turmoil, thinking of all the horrors that could have happened—a smashed port, an exploded through hull fitting, a tear in the fiberglass shell. Suddenly I felt helpless, closed in, afraid of what we would find.

I was amazed that there was no water on the cabin sole. It was all in the bilges. That was a good sign. We must not have taken much water when we rolled and apparently we hadn't split any seams. Nonetheless, I removed the heavy pillow case from one of the pillows and started packing it with cans of food that lay strewn about the cabin.

Once, when we were in New Zealand where our liferaft was being serviced, I asked Joy if she would take Jason into the raft. She said she didn't know, and the lady at the raft place said definitely not to take a cat! At the time, I asserted I would not leave without him. Now Joy eased back down into the cabin, grabbed the fingernail clippers and started cutting Jason's claws. In the struggle, she cut one too close and it bled badly.

Joy turned on the HF ham radio but it was silent. Knowing that the backstay antenna had gone down with the mast, she switched to the auxiliary. The whip antenna, amazingly, was still standing because it was attached to the radar mast which had withstood the impact from the capsize. Joy tried to broadcast a distress message, hoping the radio could send even if it couldn't receive. But we had to assume that the radio was not sending or receiving because it had taken water over it when we rolled. Joy took the EPIRB (Emergency Position Indicating Radio Beacon) off the wall, pulled out the short antenna and turned it on. The red light blinked on, indicating that it was sending its signal. That meant ships or aircraft within a radius of about 250 miles and satellites could pick up our signal and relay our position to Air and Sea Rescue.

Once the EPIRB was set off, we put on our foul weather jackets and harnesses and went topside to assess the damage. Joy was in a great deal of pain with her leg. On deck, we could see the strobe light that had been on the top of the mast, still eerily flashing underwater. As we watched, it blacked out. The electric wire severed just as if the last bit of life had left the mast. Now it was very dark. Although the wind was howling between 70 and 80 knots and the sea was mountainous, the mast over the side was acting like a drogue, greatly dampening our motion.

I had not ever seen such frightening seas! Incredulously I stared at them, not really believing my own estimate of 40 to 50 feet of height! In the face of these gigantic rollers, frequently breaking off the solid walls of sea, I felt paralyzed.

Now I know my estimate of height was probably pretty accurate. Gavin Turner, a pilot of the Queensland Government

HS 125 who participated in the search for the 35-foot Australian yacht, *Rockin' Robin,* reported the conditions as cyclonic. He said there were 30-foot swells with 20-foot waves coming off the top of them. This was in an area 300 miles south of us and thus 300 miles south of the center of the low. I read this as 50-foot seas at the *Rockin' Robin* site and therefore the seas probably were as high or higher where we were.

We crawled over the deck snapped on with our safety harnesses. Standing was not only dangerous, it was almost impossible. Even crawling against the wind was tiring. I averted my face from the wind to protect it from the rain and lashing seas. Seas high as a house were rearing up, sometimes breaking and smashing over us. The seawater felt warm.

Off to the port side, the top part of the mast, bent double and almost sheared off twelve feet above the deck, was still firmly attached to the boat with the stays and rigging. It was pounding on the teak toe rail, beginning to bite into the wood and nick the fiberglass on the side. Still attached to the broken mast, the spreaders—two aluminum poles, each about three feet long, attached to each side of the mast—were flailing about, scraping the deck and the two propane tanks. I could see the spreaders must be dodged when going forward. They swung back and forth like a guillotine ready to behead one of us or knock us overboard.

One look at the sea told me I didn't want to take to the liferaft! It would mean jumping into the water and boarding the raft from the water. Would the raft stay floating upright in these turbulent seas? It seemed unlikely. And Joy's leg worried me; she couldn't put any weight on it. If we went to the liferaft, she would have to swim or tread water (as if you could do either in such seas) and then pull herself up the liferaft boarding ladder that hangs down into the water. If she couldn't do that, it would be up to me to pull her into the raft. Could I do it? I truly didn't know. I hoped I wouldn't be put to the test. The whole idea of the raft was almost unthinkable to me.

About this time Joy was crawling back to the cockpit. She yelled over the tumultuous roar that she was going below because her leg was hurting terribly. I assured her I would be okay, not to worry.

I redirected my attention to the mast. Was there any way we could pull it aboard? Nothing left was high enough to rig an effective block and tackle to haul it up. Also, *if* we did succeed, it would probably not be safe to have on board because of our wild motion. At least the end of the mast extended out into the sea and was not pounding the hull underwater—a very dangerous situation requiring immediate action to cut it loose. That was most fortunate because it was dark as pitch. It would be much easier if we had four hands to saw through the 5/16-inch stainless steel wires holding the mast to the boat. If we attempted it now, one person would need to hold a flashlight. It was now about 2 a.m. First light was almost four hours away. Could the hull withstand four hours of pounding? One of my fears was that we would be rolled again. If so, the mast might be thrown into the hull with such force that it would rip it open.

I grabbed hold of one end of the mast that was lifting up and down banging into the boat. Pulling down on it, I found that this eliminated about two-thirds of the pounding. It also meant that the spreaders were not moving quite as much. They bothered me because I was afraid they might stave in a port. I grabbed a line and wrapped it around a section of the mast. After several attempts and some nervous seconds when the weight of the mast swept me off my feet and left me swinging precariously in midair, I finally managed to secure the line to a cleat on the lower part of the mast that was still standing to about 12 feet above the deck. This stopped much of the banging, but not all. At least with the thumping lessened, we could wait until daylight to deal with the rest.

About this time I heard a hissing sound and smelled propane. At first I thought in tying down the mast I must have inadvertently opened the valve on the large propane tank stowed on the starboard side. I tried to tighten the valve, but the hissing continued. No use wasting my time here. There was nothing I could do to prevent the gas escaping.

Next, I turned my attention to the liferaft. It was set up to be thrown off the boat from the port side and inflate when a line is pulled. This occurs when the raft is thrown overboard, leaving a line attached to *Banshee*. We certainly wouldn't want to jump out on the port side with the mast thrashing about over there. I moved the securing line of the raft over to the starboard side so we could leave from this side if we had to abandon ship. But it took monumental effort to accomplish this simple task. It meant slowly working my way to the other side of the boat. There are two hooks on my safety harness to assure that I'm always hooked onto the boat. It is a tedious task to move anywhere as it necessitates temporarily fastening one hook while searching for a place to attach the other hook. Just this one maneuver, to go from the starboard side to the port, meant about six fastenings and refastenings of my harness while bracing and moving against the violent thrashings and periodic seas washing over the boat, threatening to tear me loose and wash me overboard.

At some point, I'm not sure when, I became aware that *Nessie*, our hard dinghy which had been lashed down on the foredeck, was gone. It had probably filled with water when we rolled and sunk. It was just one more bit of evidence of our predicament. The heaviness of awful dread registered in my stomach.

I was ready now to return below. With the dodger gone, it was important to gauge accurately when to open the hatch to let myself in. Wrong timing would result in taking a wave inside. We didn't need that. Torn bits of canvas and a few bent stainless steel rods were all that remained of the dodger. Previously it gave the cockpit a lot of protection from wind and waves. Now there was nothing but tattered shreds.

When it looked safe, I quickly removed two hatch boards. It was almost impossible to keep my balance while holding onto the two boards and stepping over the low hatch board to the first step inside. Below, everything was a shambles. Having found that moving around and holding on was next to impossible with her injured leg, Joy had taken to her bunk. Already her leg was swollen to about twice its normal size and was turning a horrible shade of black, blue and green from the groin right down into her foot. Glass was strewn everywhere. I picked up pieces I could see and wiped up big globs of mayonnaise. In the process I managed to stab one finger of my right hand with a glass shard. Glass covered both mattresses so we simply turned them upside down as the underneath side was vinyl and could not harbor glass as did the fabric side.

We had already discovered that the electric bilge pump would not work. Fortunately we had a large hand pump installed under the cabin sole. All we had to do was remove the floor hatch board, insert the handle, and pump. Now we needed to see if the engine would start. Of course we couldn't use it to propel us in these conditions, nor could we use it to charge our batteries because our angle was too erratic and would prevent the oil from circulating through the engine. But still we needed to know what equipment worked and what didn't. To start the engine meant going outside to put the gears in neutral and give it some throttle. The ignition key is below. I went outside and Joy operated the key. The battery was healthy, but the engine would not fire. The motion was too severe to attempt to inspect the engine. That job would have to wait until another time. This information told us that we would have to use electricity carefully. We turned off the refrigerator, but left the satnav going. It was important to keep track of where we were. Possibly the radio would become operative again and, when we made contact, we could give our position. Regardless of whether or not we had a radio, knowing our position was important.

Joy sprayed the ham radio with WD 40 and periodically tried to broadcast. Each time she turned it on, we fervently hoped it would receive, but each time we were disappointed by utter silence. Nevertheless Joy tried transmitting, just on the vague chance that it would get out.

Meanwhile as time passed, we could safely assume we were not taking on water except when heavy seas smashed over us. When this occurred, one of us would sit on the floor and hand pump the bilge.

Time dragged. We watched the clock—almost living for 6 a.m. when Derek would realize something had happened and, we hoped, notify the authorities. The boat seemed not to be leaking and gradually our confidence in *Banshee's* seaworthiness was being restored.

It was 5:45 a.m. The first weak light filtered through a gray sky—time to go outside and cope with the wayward mast. Each pound of it against the hull reminded us that it could hole us and then we would be forced to take the liferaft. Both of us knew such a move would be dangerous, even life threatening; those seas promised nothing but danger, discomfort and a greatly diminished chance of being found and rescued. We had always said, "Step up to get into your liferaft," meaning, only get into the raft when the boat is sinking. We knew our chances for survival and being found were much better in a boat than in a raft. Also, there is no way to propel a raft. You are simply captive, drifting wherever the raft goes, no longer the master of your fate.

In the light of dawn we suited up in foul weather jackets and stepped out into the cockpit. Joy had downed a strong pain killer so she could work on deck. As soon as I pulled myself up the companionway steps into the cockpit, I noticed that my thighs felt like water, as if my strength just flowed out my legs. I thought I was going to faint. I couldn't go on deck. I realized I was in shock. I told Joy. I had to go below and lie down! I retreated and she did too. Just barely conscious, I collapsed onto a bunk amidst clutter and disarray. For about five minutes I lay there, trying to relax and regain my strength.

Finally I pulled myself up the steps and into the cockpit, but once again, the strength flowed out of my body. Again I hastened below and dropped onto the bunk. Joy said her arms and hands were paralyzed, frozen in shock. She too lay down on the bunk, her head at my feet. We lay there too weak to talk. I closed my eyes and waited. It was the thought of where we were, 450 miles offshore with no mast, no way to propel ourselves that hit me over and over in waves. Finally I told myself, "You have to go up and take care of the mast. Your life depends on it!"

Both of us succeeded this time in going topside and crawling along the deck to inspect everything for the first time in sufficient light. The mast had bent in two places, several feet below the spreaders and several feet above them. Tying off one end of the mast had caused it to break off entirely, which was a stroke of luck because, otherwise, we would have had to saw through the mast itself and the stainless steel track on the mast. Sawing the mast in addition to eight stays would have been very nearly impossible. Also, how would we have been able to reach and steady ourselves to saw on the bent area of the mast which was 12 feet off the deck? All the stays and shrouds of 5/16-inch stainless steel were intact. Not one of them had failed. The spinnaker pole, formerly attached to the mast, had lost one end and what remained was mangled. It would be advantageous if we could pull the mast wreckage aboard and save the roller furling. Also, saving all the upper Sta-Lok fittings would save us money in the long run—if we saved *Banshee.*

Unfortunately, saving anything was out of the question. The Pro-Furl with the genny, the storm jib, the mast and all the fittings were extremely heavy. The section of mast over the side had also filled with water. Winds of 70 to 80 knots with breaking seas made pulling anything aboard not only dangerous, but simply impossible. We would have to cut the stays. Neither of us was strong enough to cut them with bolt cutters. We would have to saw them laboriously with a hacksaw!

We noticed that one of the stays was draped over the break in the mast. Because of its position, it would have to be the last wire cut loose. If it was cut first while the other stays were attached, the released pressure from cutting this stay would catapult the mast into the side of the boat.

I held the wire for Joy to try and stabilize it against the raucous motion while she attacked it with the hacksaw we had brought topside with us.

"Damn," Joy shouted, "it's dull, wouldn't cut butter."

"Sit tight. I'll go find a new blade." I suddenly remembered— I had just bought two new blades before we left Manly. Premonition?

Slowly I fought my way back to the cockpit. Just as I got there and was about to fasten the second clasp on my safety line to a place inside the cockpit, a white growler broke over us. Tons of water washed over me flattening me to the decks which were awash. Frothing white water had filled the cockpit and was cascading from the decks down to the swirling maelstrom. For a moment I thought the cockpit drains were plugged because the water didn't appear to be draining out. But gradually it began to subside. I could only hope we wouldn't be assaulted again before the water drained out. Fortunately it didn't hit us when I had the hatch open. I looked to see if Joy was okay. She was clipped on, sitting wedged between the side of the house and the net on the lifelines, clutching tightly to the handrail.

Below, I had to clear away the clutter so I could open the locker where the blades were stowed. I didn't even think about the fact that I was bedraggled and barefoot. Somewhere between the companionway steps and the locker, I stepped on a piece of glass. It was one of the long slivers from the lamp glass. Luckily I was able to remove it with my fingers. When I opened the locker, tools flew out, the vise barely missing my hand. Finally, after digging, I found the two new blades. Better only take one topside with me. I would come back when we needed the other. I couldn't risk losing it.

Laboriously, I made my way back to Joy. With both of us wedged firmly, we kept two hands on the saw while Joy removed the old blade and tightened the new one in place.

We set to work. It wasn't easy. With the deck rolling, wind howling and seas pounding, it required trying to hold ourselves on board while at the same time attempting to hold the wire and saw it. We started with the most difficult stays, the one upper and two lowers on the starboard side. This place was in direct whacking range of the flailing spreaders. This was also the high side which took the brunt of breaking seas. At first I tried to do it myself, knowing I was more agile than Joy with her injured leg. Soon it became apparent that this job could only be done with two sets of hands. After watching the arc of the flailing spreaders closely, we sat just outside the area with perhaps two inches to spare. Finally the last of the three stays let go.

Next we had to move to the port side. Moving around the deck in storm conditions is difficult at the best of times. With the mast down, it was mayhem. A tangle of ropes and wire cable lay over the deck and cabintop. To cross this jumbled network, we had to keep snapping and unsnapping our safety harnesses to move at all. It took so much time, crawling, holding against the motion and positioning the safety harnesses. It was also exhausting. Somehow despite all these difficulties, we finally got to the port side so we could begin sawing the three stays there. Being the low side, it was really easier to manage, and Joy felt she could do it on her own while I moved about the deck cutting lines. This meant another trip below for me to get the fishing knife, the one knife I always keep razor sharp for emergencies. There were about thirty lines to cut loose, as these too were keeping the mast attached to the boat. I got below and up on deck again without incident.

But before Joy had finished releasing the port shrouds, a squall increased the wind to between 90 and 100 knots. It blew so hard it simply flattened the crests of the towering seas and picked up the surface water in sheets. There was no visibility as the seawater filled the air like a snow blizzard. As quickly as we could, we retreated below. With that tremendous wind, I believe we could have been blown overboard if we remained on deck.

This nasty squall blew for about ten minutes before subsiding.

When we went back outside, we started sawing away the backstay. The stern of the boat was chaotic. The port solar panel, which was on the low side of the boat when we were capsized, had been pushed off its mount at the base. It landed wedged in behind the wheel. I was amazed to see it had not been smashed because it is glass. The horseshoe buoy had fallen into the water and its line was tightly wound around the windvane. The line had entangled a small gasoline fuel can which was floating just aft. The canvas side panels lashed to the lifelines in the cockpit were torn and some areas were shredded. A million lines lay in a snarled heap in the cockpit, but it was no time to be concerned with them. We had to press on to abort the mast. That was still the first order of business.

Once the backstay was severed, we crawled forward, this time all the way to the bow to decide how we were going to cope with the roller furling. I didn't like the prospect of trying to saw through the rolled-up sail, the aluminum extrusion and the 5/16-inch wire. Better to release the bolt holding through the toggle. First I had to remove the nuts at each end with two wrenches. Then Joy gave me a hammer and screwdriver so I could pound the bolt out. But the strain on the toggle was tremendous, preventing it from coming out. Periodically the pressure lessened as a wave lifted us up. I would have to coordinate my efforts with the motion of the seas.

In my frustration I kept yelling back to Joy, "It won't come loose. I'm hitting for all I'm worth, but I don't think I can get it!"

"You have to. Hit it again. Keep it up. Damn it, Jeannine. You have to get it free. You have to. You have to." She kept shouting.

Finally—I think I was lucky—it came loose. With this, the mast should have fallen into the water because Joy had cut loose the port stays and I had cut all the ropes. But it didn't fall free. Somehow Joy had overlooked one port stay. It was down in the water with the weight of the mast tugging at it. We had to reach into the water and pull the metal stay up. I held while she sawed. All this was overboard. We held our only hacksaw overboard without a lanyard. How stupid. We should have had lanyards on all our tools. We could have lost them overboard. Fortunately we didn't. And, miraculously, we had sawed through eight 5/16-inch stays using only one blade! And, even more amazingly, we did not break the blade! Even on land we usually break blades by twisting them. Lady Luck had been with us.

All of the cutting and hacking had been necessary, yet it was painful to destroy the rigging we had installed with our own hands only a little over a year before. I almost cried as I watched the newly installed ProFurl slide into the deep. We had waited a long time to get roller furling and now after using it perhaps only six times, it was lost. Momentarily we had just dumped about eight to ten thousand dollars into the sea. Sadly we knew that the bottom line was that our lives were more important than our gear. Three hours and fifteen minutes after we started, the job of freeing the mast was completed.

It was 9:15 by the time we had cleared the decks of our rigging and retreated below. Time enough for Penta Comstat to have notified Sea Safety that we must be in trouble. The day passed slowly as we waited, hoping to hear the drone of approaching engines. But we heard nothing. Maybe Derek didn't report us. Was he waiting for the afternoon roll call before telling anyone we were in some kind of trouble?

Unknown to us, the wheels had already started turning on land. When Penta Comstat was unable to contact us at 0600 hours, they advised Sea Safety in Canberra. When we also didn't come up on the normal 0800 hours schedule, Derek was certain we had a real problem. But it was still another six hours before a passing aircraft picked up an EPIRB just after midday and notified Sea Safety who issued a MARSAR (Marine Air Reconnaissance Search and Rescue). Because of Penta Comstat's notification of our position from the previous evening radio contact, Sea Safety had no problem ascertaining that the signal had to be coming from *Banshee*.

Our spirits were flagging when suddenly around 2:30 p.m. we heard a plane. Hurrying topside, I waved my arms in a mayday signal to a circling Royal Australian Air Force (RAAF) Orion flying very low. Surely they must see me. Joy was so excited she ignored her pain and hobbled up the steps and began waving too.

Eventually the plane left. We had been spotted and we were confident a helicopter would appear soon and we would be lifted off. But nothing happened until just before dark, around 5 p.m., when a second plane appeared, a Search Air Rescue Gulfstream jet, flew over, circling many times and dropping two rafts. The liferaft drifted down next to us, upside down. There was a sign printed on it saying "BOARD HERE." Several hundred yards away was another smaller type of raft carrying a light.

We were puzzled. What did they want? Surely they didn't expect us to climb into the raft. We couldn't right a ten-person raft anyway, not in these conditions and especially not when our boat was intact. Unfortunately we couldn't communicate by VHF radio as ours was no longer functioning. It too had got a saltwater bath in the roll. We didn't learn until later that most aircraft do not have a VHF with channels compatible with VHF on boats anyway. Why didn't they drop us some kind of message or a two-way radio? Disappointed and with sinking spirits, we watched the Gulfstream turn away. It was swallowed up by the darkening gray sky as night descended.

I told Joy I thought I should attempt to tie the upside down raft to the boat. Perhaps they had some kind of radio beacon on the raft to track us.

She became very fearful. "Don't you dare try to pick up the line from the raft. It's too far out. And in these terrible seas, you could fall overboard. Then where would we be? You couldn't get back aboard *Banshee* and you can't get into an upside down raft. You would be dead and I might too because I can't do much with this damn leg."

"But this might be the only way they can find us again," I pleaded.

"No. Absolutely not. Leave it alone. Please."

In the end I relented. It was too risky. I left the raft alone.

It was our first night, disabled, drifting, still in the throes of horrendous weather. We could only hope *Banshee* would continue to protect us, that we would not be rolled again. We had no lights to carry at night. We had to keep watch. If we saw a ship, we could fire off a flare. The EPIRB's light was still glowing, still transmitting, we thought, but we turned it off during the darkness to save batteries. Enclosed in total blackness, we drifted and drifted through the night.

Chapter 3

Adrift

Night comes early in June in the Southern Hemisphere. Since we needed to conserve our power, once night came we sat in darkness. Without a mast to stabilize the boat, the motion was terrible and darkness only seemed to exaggerate the movement. The gimballed stove swung the full distance of its arc, thrashing back and forth so quickly that the most we dared to do was boil water in a kettle. Even then I held the handle to prevent it from leaping off the stove and sloshing scalding water over us. Holding the kettle, I stood off to the side of the stove to avoid being struck during its mad gyrations.

Most meals consisted of instant cereal my mother had sent us. Occasionally during the ordeal, as on this evening, we ate a cold can of beans. Once in a while we drank a cup of instant coffee or tea, but mostly we drank Gatorade, a dry powder mixed with water that contains the necessary nutrients for replenishing the body's electrolytes, and water. We consumed a fair amount of liquids, but neither of us had an appetite.

Amazingly, we weren't seasick. Never once throughout the entire episode did either of us experience any queasiness.

A 12-hour night in these surroundings passes very slowly. Without lights there was little we could do but talk about the prospects of being found and rescued, saving our boat, and failing being found, what we could do when the weather calmed down. With so much time on our hands, we had pretty much exhausted all our thoughts and feelings about our situation. We had no fears about imminent danger. If not found in the next few days, there were several scenarios that could transpire. The worst one was being hit by another storm and sustaining damage that would sink the boat. I have read accounts of people spending up to four months adrift in a liferaft. The Baileys survived for 119 days in a liferaft. Still, as I told Joy, the most frightening thing to me about shipwreck has been going to a raft.

Another scenario was drifting on in *Banshee*, but not being able—because of continued rough weather—to jury rig her and sail her to land. Somewhere we might end up on a reef or a deserted island and spend months trying to survive, hoping to be found eventually.

The inside of the boat was depressing because of the clutter and pervasive dampness. I straightened up as much as I could, but in many cases the effort was futile because the incessant tossing from beam to beam threw things back to the floor. From the head forward to the bow was a morass of soggy books, magazines, assorted papers, bedding, blankets and clothing. I should have just discarded the entire mess overboard, but it required too much energy, so I confined my efforts to tidying up our immediate living area, the main saloon. Joy had her bunk on the starboard side, mine was on the port.

I think the loss of sleep, tremendous exertion, and the constant wild motion were the factors most responsible for our general depression. In Joy's case, her pain and the heavy medication were additional elements contributing to her emotional state.

Much of our bedding was drenched; some of it I tossed out because it was full of glass. What remained was very damp and salty. We could squeeze water out of one feather pillow and the other two were hardly better, but that's all we had. Most of our clothes were damp, others soaking wet. With everything closed up, the humidity and heat created the perfect environment for mold. After 24 hours with the refrigerator off, I had to discard most of its contents. At sea we do not throw plastic into the water, but now we had to ignore this environmental concern because the plastic wrappers on rotting meat could not be left aboard in these circumstances.

During the daylight hours on June 7, as the center of the low passed over us, the wind diminished. Consequently the seas lost some of their sledgehammer punch, but by night conditions worsened again, becoming almost as bad as during the previous night when we were capsized. As the center moved off, we got the other side of the cyclone where the wind began to howl again. In the center the barometric pressure dropped to 995 millibars.

Joy's biggest fear during this night was being run down by a ship. I felt the chances of this happening were minimal. Each of us took two-hour watches through the night to keep a lookout for ships and to hand pump the bilge every hour.

By daybreak on Friday, June 8, we were in pretty good spirits, feeling confident rescuers would appear at first light or soon thereafter. Since the last plane found us the previous evening, we had only moved ten miles. The Walker satnav was still working and periodically we plotted our position. The satnav was calculating our drift at about half a knot. By now the wind had gone southeasterly so we were drifting northwesterly. Considering we hadn't moved very far, I couldn't see there would be any problem locating us again.

At first light I looked out to see if I could spot either of the rafts that had been deployed. They were nowhere in sight. That was not surprising as my vision was severely limited by monumental, turbulent seas that went hissing by, frothing with foam. The rafts could have been as close as several hundred yards and I would not have been able to see them from the deck. But having a different rate of drift from us, I would expect the rafts to be some distance away.

It got to be 8 a.m., then 9 and was approaching 10 o'clock. No sign of anyone. Joy was becoming rather alarmed about it and I said, hoping to reassure her, it might take time to find us because visibility was not very good. But then we had our EPIRB on and they should be able to locate us from its signal. I was concerned about conditions which were still quite severe. It was cloudy, sometimes raining, and mountainous seas were still breaking. In these conditions it would be very difficult to detect us from the air.

To increase our visibility, I went on deck, wearing my harness, and tied two red blankets across the boom. I wished for a cloth of international orange, but unfortunately we didn't have one. Red blankets were the only bright color we had. While on deck I also adjusted the starboard solar panel so it would give our batteries a bit of a charge. This maneuver was actually more hazardous than attaching the blankets. On deck when a sea broke over us, I could lie flat holding on to stanchions or a hand rail, and the net strung onto the lifelines acted as a reassuring safety net.

The solar panel was a different matter altogether. In order to reach the screw for adjusting its angle, I had to stand on the cockpit lazarette and, as the boat lurched and tossed about or if a breaking sea caught us, I was in danger of being flung overboard. It was extremely hard to balance and I really needed two hands to adjust the panel and two more to hold on. I wrapped my arms around the stern gallows in an effort to hold on but my wrists and arms took a real beating when the boat tossed back and forth. Because of the difficulty of this procedure, I only adjusted it twice each day, which meant that we did not get the optimum charging from the panel.

Just before 10 a.m., it suddenly occurred to me that we ought to see if our transistor radio could receive. Perhaps we could learn something on the news. We turned it on and were ecstatic when it blared out some loud music. It was the Rockhampton ABC station. The first item on the news reported that two yachts off the Queensland coast were in distress. The first one was *Rockin' Robin* with four male crew, the second was *Banshee* with two American yachtswomen. (At least they weren't calling us *girls*.) We wondered how they knew the name of the boat and who we were. We learned that rescue operations had been hampered the previous day because there were no long range helicopters in Rockhampton and because conditions were sometimes too severe for aircraft to fly. Long range helicopters were being brought to Rockhampton from the Townsville Army Base. We cheered. And cried.

But the 11 a.m. news dashed our newly raised hopes. Spotter planes had gone directly out to one of the rafts they had dropped to us, but they had not seen *Banshee*.

As we later learned from newsman John Ryan, a Super Kingair aircraft, commanded by Captain Alister Buckingham, left Rockhampton at dawn to relocate *Banshee*. Captain Buckingham told John Ryan, "We flew straight to the radio beacon. The radio signal was loud and clear on both frequencies. But when we got there, we could only see the upturned liferaft two miles away from the beacon. There was no sign of the yacht. We had lost her!" Captain Buckingham wanted to keep looking for us, but he was told give up the search and return to the base.

Strangely this information differs from what Sea Safety reported. They said the search that day failed to locate any sign of the *Banshee*, liferaft or survivors. If it is true that the liferaft was never sighted during the search effort, it only reconfirms our opinion that boarding the raft would have been futile!

June 8 was not only a bad time for us, this day was when *Rockin' Robin* first got into trouble. In the early hours they put out a distress call which was noted by Sea Safety. *Rockin' Robin* reported taking on water. That was at 1:16 a.m. when the yacht was roughly 500 miles east of Bundaberg. They reported two feet of water through the boat which they had bailed down to 14 inches. The crew thought it was under control, but then they said they would have to abandon ship. They put out a full mayday at 1:52 a.m., reporting the wind as 40 knots. At 2:07 a.m., a RAAF aircraft Orion 251 was diverted from the *Banshee* search. The Orion arrived on site at 6:30 a.m. and dropped an Air Sea Rescue Kit to *Rockin' Robin*.

The 11 a.m. news report also said it was feared that one or both of us on the *Banshee* might be injured and that we might have taken to the liferaft! (Note: this information contradicts what the pilot reported.) The plane that had spotted us on the previous day had only seen one person aboard *Banshee*. The bit about the liferaft bothered us. Why would they assume we had taken to a raft? They had seen our boat floating high in the water only hours earlier. Why would we take to a raft?

Our main concern at this point and throughout our ordeal was Joy's leg. It was looking very bad. She couldn't put any weight on it and it was more than twice its normal size. By now her entire leg was discolored, a deep shade of black. Joy was afraid of having a clot migrate to her brain. It would mean immediate death. I wanted her to stay off her leg and I undertook all necessary activities in order to keep her immobilized.

As the day wore on and no rescue craft appeared, our spirits fell. Worse yet, on the 5 p.m. news, they said they had lost our EPIRB signal! That was no good. The batteries must have died.

Joy might have physically been incapacitated, but it didn't affect her mind. She instantly came up with the idea of seeing if we could wire the EPIRB into one of our ship's batteries. That would, of course, depend on the voltage required. We wouldn't want to hook it up to something too powerful; it would blow up the EPIRB.

We pulled out the specs on the EPIRB (a Narco) and were astonished to learn that it was expected to operate for only *one* continuous hour! Now what good is an emergency beacon that only operates for one hour? How distressing.

Months after returning to land, we once again found the literature on the Narco EPIRB. It does not say it will only operate for one continuous hour. Instead it states the EPIRB has "sufficient battery power to transmit continuously for 8 days at 21 degrees C." In the midst of the confusion, Joy simply misread something. Since the signal was no longer being picked up, we assumed the EPIRB had stopped working, although its light was still on. Because the signal was not picked up for several days even after it was wired into our ship's battery, we don't know if the batteries with the set were still operable.

The EPIRB was packaged to float and be waterproof. Periodically we have to send it back to the States to have its batteries serviced by the manufacturer. We had talked about purchasing a new one, one that could be user serviced. Now here we were with this thing. I was feeling angry and upset that we hadn't bought a new one. Disappointingly the specs said nothing about required voltage. That meant we had to tear the damn thing apart.

We removed the top part containing the printed circuit board and the antenna, disconnecting it from the battery pack. The warning on the case—"Warranty invalid if removed"—would have been laughable if not so serious. The bottom part of the EPIRB contained the battery pack which had been sealed inside a heavy plastic case with some super black glue. I took the hammer and chisel to it and began hacking away with a vengeance.

There were nine D-cell batteries in the pack. Tediously I peeled away the black glue so we could read the descriptions on the batteries. They were nicads. Finally, using a volt meter, Joy determined that at full charge these batteries would produce 13.5 volts. Our engine starting battery was fully charged.

To have access to the engine battery, we had to remove the companionway steps and the engine cover. With the extreme motion, it took both of us to handle the steps and the cover, which are heavy and bulky. Now Joy had to lean over the front of the engine to reach the battery. She was surprised to discover that in the capsize this battery, despite being tied down, had fallen over and was leaning against the engine fuel line. Miraculously, it hadn't dented the copper tubing.

I was concerned that Joy had to be up on her feet to wire in the EPIRB, but there was no other alternative. My arms were too short to reach the battery. Joy attached the wires and the red light for the EPIRB glowed! Success. If we had known it then, we could have tested to see if it was putting out a signal by turning the FM dial on our transistor to 100 Mhz. We didn't know and just had to trust that it was signalling.

June 9 was a Saturday. On the 7 a.m. news we were ecstatic when we heard the search for us and *Rockin' Robin* was being intensified. Sixteen planes were going to search with 50 observers. Later we heard that 20 planes joined in the search.

Once again I went out on deck to tie on the red blankets. I noticed the clouds were breaking up, which meant improved visibility. Even the seas were down a bit. Everywhere I looked in the sky there were rainbows. It was phenomenal! I considered it a sign that today we would be rescued.

The day advanced and frequently one or the other of us would think we heard a plane. I would crack open the hatch and look out only to see a cloud-filled sky and a blue-gray ocean awash with white frothy seas. It was diabolical how the wind mimicked the sound of an aircraft. Once Joy was so insistent that she heard aircraft I fired off a smoke flare to appease her. The exercise was instructive. Immediately it was apparent that these little 6-inch flares were useless. In these winds—40 to 45 knots—the smoke was instantly swallowed by the seas! The smoke dispersed instantly. The flare lasted less than a minute and would not have been visible even 100 feet away. Now I knew that if we saw something, I'd better fire off a parachute flare. Unfortunately we only had two of them.

Joy was suffering in pain with her leg. She was sometimes afraid of the consequences of not being found so she could have proper medical attention. I was very apprehensive and knew of nothing I could do to help her. Now the formation of a clot was not the only fear. What would we do if she developed gangrene? While we carried on board a local anesthetic, sutures, and two medical texts which describe all types of medical procedures, I had difficulty imagining how I could perform an amputation. How many times had we both wished Joy had not been injured? Without this complication, most of our concerns would be lessened. With calm weather and two able bodied people, we could easily jury rig *Banshee*. That also seemed to be the only way we could save our boat. If we abandoned her, she would be gone.

Our bags were packed and sitting in the middle of the cabin sole. They consisted of two small backpacks and one seabag. We'd had many discussions about what to take if we were rescued. And many questions. Could *Banshee* be salvaged? We wondered and talked about various friends, what they would think and feel knowing we were out here. We wondered if the news had reached the States? Did our mothers know? We hoped not. We didn't want them to worry. I wished many times we had a way to send a message to let everyone know we were okay. I kept thinking about things I would do when I got back to land, only to remind myself that I was thinking about a future that I might not have.

Such thoughts always brought me back to thinking about jury rigging. Joy and I had agreed we would not attempt jury rigging until conditions settled down and not before they called off the search. We knew that the search would be based on our direction and rate of drift. If we redirected our course, as we would when we began sailing, they would never find us.

Our position at 3:12 p.m. on Saturday was 20° 40'.578S by 156° 11'.55E. Since Thursday we had moved only 45 miles.

Again on the 5 p.m. news we heard that the search had intensified. We hugged each other and cried. We were surprised to learn that the four crew from *Rockin' Robin* had not been rescued. An earlier broadcast had made it sound as if their rescue was imminent. It said that *Rockin' Robin* was sinking and the men abandoned her going into a ten-man raft that was dropped to them. Two rafts were dropped and we first heard that three men had gone to one raft and one to another. The entire operation was seen and photographed from the air. A French frigate, *Admiral Charner*, was supposedly standing by and would pick them up soon. Later we learned that the ship was 20 hours away.

For the first time on Saturday I felt we were beginning to emerge from the sense of shock and loss. I felt a kind of distancing from *Banshee*. She was wet, in total disarray—so different from her normal state. I believe I was preparing myself emotionally for leaving and losing *Banshee*.

On the evening news we heard that they had found some wreckage which they thought was from *Banshee:* a yellow drum, a radar reflector and a navigation light. How silly, we both said. Sighting wreckage doesn't mean a boat has sunk! Of course they would find items that were swept overboard. We'd lost many things from the deck and many others when we cut loose the mast. We did not own a yellow drum, however. Our hearts sank when we heard that hopes of finding us were dimming. They thought we were gone!

Joy and I were appalled. How could they think life could go so easily. We were still here, very much alive. If they followed the direction that the wind pushed us, they would surely find us. Both of us were certain they were not searching in the right place. If so, they would have found us by now. And why were they not hearing our EPIRB? Since wiring it into the ship's battery, we let it run all day, shutting it down only at night to conserve energy at a time they would not be searching for us.

We talked about how long they would continue a search for us. Joy thought at least a week. I disagreed. When they're talking about wreckage and hopes dimming, that means they are nearing the end of the search. I told Joy I felt certain the next day, Sunday, June 10, would be the final day of the search. If they didn't find us then, they would call it off. We would be on our own.

That night on my watch I thought in greater detail how we could jury rig *Banshee*. Luckily there was still about 12 feet of mast above the deck. We could extend it by lashing the boom to the mast stump using hose clamps as fasteners and line for additional lashing. The method for raising the boom, which at first had seemed an intimidating chore, came to me in a flash. We could run a line attached to the boom over the top of the stump and then hoist the boom up by using the hand windlass. What a beautiful solution. Before raising it, though, we would need to attach all our lines to the boom that would be used for stays and halyards. With this rig we could also fly two sails—the staysail forward and the trysail from the boom. We still had part of the trysail track on the mast stump. The sail could not be raised as high as normally, but it would still work. With two sails we could even tack to windward, so the boat would be quite maneuverable.

A major concern was that we had lost the windvane's water paddle. This meant we would have to hand steer, a very tiring activity since we had a minimum of 500 miles to sail; but if we had to tack our way back, the distance could be double. We could only use the autopilot in the event we could start the engine and charge the batteries. Joy and I had already determined a geographic point at which we had to sail for land, otherwise with prevailing southeasterlies, if we got too far north we would end up heading straight into Great Barrier Reef. Our goal would be to come into Australia just south of the reef, making Gladstone.

Jury rigging and sailing *Banshee* back was the most appealing plan. In fact this appeared to be the only way we could save *Banshee*. If we were rescued it seemed highly unlikely that *Banshee* could be salvaged. She was so far offshore, a salvage operation would be next to impossible. Additionally, we simply didn't have the funds to pay someone to salvage her. Perhaps more importantly, it's a matter of pride and good seamanship to take care of yourself and get your vessel back to port.

The only drawback was Joy's leg. She needed immediate medical attention. It could develop into a life-or-death situation. The black and blue color indicated massive internal bleeding and if she had just one scratch, the danger of gangrene was very real. If we sailed back, it would be days, maybe even a couple of weeks before making land. That's a long time with the kind of medical problem Joy faced. Joy would be unable to do much physically, so that left me to do most of the jury rigging alone. I believed I could do it, but the weather would have to calm down first.

We were concerned about the condition of the rudder. Joy thought it was damaged, but I thought it was not. After being rolled, I had tried to keep the wheel braked so the rudder would not thrash violently back and forth, but the brake would not hold it against the omnipotence of the sea. Consequently, the wheel was rapidly spinning most of the time.

The port solar panel was trapped behind the wheel and would have to be moved before one could steer. Each day we talked about remounting the panel and plugging it in so as to get more charging. But conditions were just too rough and the panel too awkward and heavy to attempt it. So it lay there behind the wheel. I tied it down with a line just in case we got knocked down or capsized again.

Food was no problem. We had enough for a year, perhaps longer. For fresh foods we had plenty of dried beans, grains and seeds which could be sprouted. We had a three month supply of multivitamins and minerals. Fresh water would not be a problem. We still had more than 30 gallons and we could always catch rainwater.

I felt fairly optimistic, except for Joy's leg. If we had to go it alone, the probability of surviving and getting ourselves back to land was good. We needed settled weather to rig though and, with a jury rig, I wouldn't want to encounter heavy conditions. Bad weather could lash us again before we reached Australia. The hull had taken a real bashing for several days. There was no way of knowing what damage another roll could inflict—the opening of a seam, smashing in a port or tearing off a hatch. These were some of the thoughts and feelings we discussed Saturday night and some I continued to think about during my solitary watch.

Chapter 4

Rescued

Two very strange things occurred during our last night adrift. The first was that my side of the boat, which had been the low side, suddenly became the high side. I asked Joy what had happened? Had the wind shifted 180 degrees? I poked my head up the hatch to check the wind direction. It was still southeasterly. That meant we had turned 180 degrees, not the wind! The only explanation was that one of the massive seas had picked us up and turned us around! Most curious, but also frightening when you think about it. Without any sail up and not making any way, we were like a cork, bobbing at the will of the aqueous surge.

During the early morning hours, the second weird thing took place. I became aware of a profound change in the boat's motion. Previously it had been rather boisterous and rolly, and there was still the occasional drop into a trough as we simply came to a void with no water under our keel. Now it was as if the sea had flattened out. I could hear the sound of lapping water, as opposed to the roar of breakers and racing swells. I felt short, sharp slaps against the hull.

I opened the hatch and peered out. The wind was still blowing about 30 knots, but the breaking seas were gone and so were the swells. The surface was heaped up in a succession of pyramids forming sharp peaks. Hence the slapping sounds. The clouds had cleared enough that the moon illuminated the strange scene, lending it an unreal, ethereal cast. What was going on? Were we over a reef? Going onto a reef? I could see there was a very strong current and it was whipping past us at an incredible speed. It was opposing the wind which probably accounted for the triangular shaped waves, but I could not understand what had happened to the huge swells and waves we had had. The wavelet slapping continued for about 45 minutes and then conditions resumed their previous characteristics.

Banshee, before the storm with all sails set, as we left Manly, Australia for Vanuatu.

After being storm-tossed, capsized, dismasted, abandoned in mid-ocean and towed behind a motor vessel, *Banshee* looks battered and bedraggled. We survey the damage as *Banshee* motors to the dock in Townsville.

Seen from the deck of the *Maersk Sentosa*, *Banshee* is not easy to spot amid large foaming whitecaps.

Slowly and carefully Captain Bob Fisher eases the huge ship alongside *Banshee*. One of the crew tossed me a giant hawser.

Held together by the hawser and two more lines, *Banshee* and *Maersk Sentosa* sawed up and down at different rates, slamming together with scraping and crunching sounds. I was grateful we were being rescued but I had to fight the feeling of wanting to push us off from this monster which seemed to be killing *Banshee*.

With the mayor of Rockhampton at the Rockhampton Show Days, we thanked the people of Australia for our rescue. From the time we landed in this wonderful city, where we were graciously welcomed and generously helped, we were also given a great deal of media attention. Television newscasts continued to broadcast the details of our rescue and we were interviewed extensively by TV, radio and newspaper journalists.

Joy rests her injured leg during the program.

We were meeting the press in Rockhampton the day after our rescue wearing clothing donated to us by the Australian Red Cross.

Jason, our cat. One Australian newspaper dubbed him the $2 million cat, explaining that he nearly foiled the rescue when Joy refused to be winched aboard the helicopter without him.

Joy and I answer phone calls and messages in the office loaned to us by the answering service in Rockhampton.

The two Blackhawks that plucked us from the deck of the *Maersk Sentosa* logged a record distance for the helicopters. They had never flown so far. Even with extra fuel loaded aboard, the crew was uncertain if they had enough to get back to Rockhampton.

Banshee's rescue vessel, the *Saramoa*, slides into her berth beside us in Townsville.

Joy and I are photographed for Brisbane's *Courier-Mail* with *Banshee's* rescuers Bob Bedford, behind Joy, Mike Carney, who donated fuel for the Saramoa's salvage expedition, and George Collins, center. The newspaper story related how burly George, a former Navy diver, swam without a safety line to attach the tow rope to the *Banshee* and how Bob and George battled gale-force winds and mountainous seas to tow *Banshee* back to safety.

Getting *Banshee* berthed before we start to clean up.

Her port toerail was lifted and the hull and deck separated when coming alongside the *Maersk Sentosa*. The bow pulpit and port light were smashed at the same time. The stanchons were bent by the mast as it hung over the side and pounded the hull, chipping fiberglass.

Jason peers down
into the cabin.

Banshee berthed
in Townsville,
damaged and in
disarray. The wind
generator was
shattered and the
windvane broken.
Though the canvas
stayed attached to
the stern rail, the
dodger was
entirely washed
off the deck.

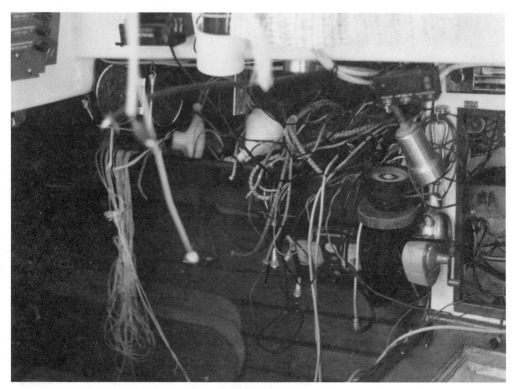

What a mess inside! Above, after we pulled out the electronics. Below, canned goods made rusty stains in the lockers.

Above, looking forward into the chain locker after everything was stripped out.
Below, looking aft. At this point the task of rebuilding seemed endless.

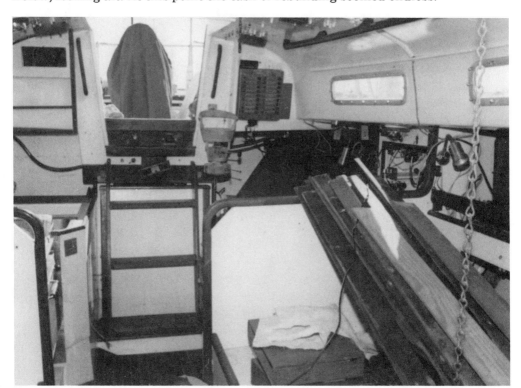

Banshee is loaded on the trailer truck that hauled her from Townsville down to Mooloolaba and Lawrie's Marina, a trip of nearly 800 miles.

The damaged toerail was stripped off so that shiprights Peter Creese, Steve Miller and Ray Seddon could rejoin the hull and the deck and bend on a new teak replacement.

Our dear friend Frank Anderson helped us physically and emotionally throughout the task of rebuilding.

After four months on the hard at Lawrie' s Marina, *Banshee* is ready to go back to her element.

But not before one last coat of bottom paint.

John Biggers and the veterinarian monitor Jason's first steps ashore after his release from nine months of quarantine.

With the work finished, we take *Banshee* out on a shakedown cruise with the new roller furling genny. We incorporated a hard top in the new dodger for strength. This also offers more protection than the old one did and gives it a squarish shape. Everything has been redone, rebuilt, strengthened, honed and fine tuned. We are more than ready to go cruising again!

Sunday morning, June 10, dawned clear with deep blue rolling seas stretching to meet a cerulean sky. Until about 8 a.m. the wind had eased, but once the sun drove off the night chill, the wind sprang back up to 35 knots. The rough seas would make it formidable to spot us amidst large foaming whitecaps. I wasn't feeling very optimistic about being found because by now we were convinced that they were searching in the wrong place and, for some reason, still not picking up our EPIRB signal. I tried not to let Joy see how I felt.

I knew she was feeling very depressed and concerned about her leg. She had requested that we not turn the radio on at 7 a.m. as had become our practice. The news release the previous day had ended on such a pessimistic note she didn't want to hear anymore doom and gloom about our being lost, and I thought she really feared they would say the search was being abandoned.

Even though we had eaten little for the last three days, some dirty dishes had accumulated. Just before 10 a.m., I started to wash them when suddenly a thunderous blast sounded overhead. Immediately I tore open the main hatch and charged up the steps. Almost directly overhead, flying low, a jet streaked past! Did they see us? I watched them diminish to a mere speck before they banked and turned back, but it appeared they were flying another leg of a search grid and were not coming back anywhere near us. Joy handed me a parachute flare and I waited until they seemed close enough. Pointing it downwind and skyward, I pulled the plug. It exploded with a horrifying blast and soared upward, glowing bright red and leaving a smoke plume behind.

Surely it was an eternity, but at last the plane veered from its course, circled wide and headed toward us. Both of us stood in the cockpit frantically waving our arms, shouting and crying at the same time and hugging each other. The jet made several passes, gradually slowing.

Within half an hour, three spotter planes were circling, dropping smoke flares in a wide ring about us along with floating buoys. This time they were not going to lose us!

We were going to be rescued! We were going to leave *Banshee*. The decision had been made.

Our minds racing, we were trying to do everything at once: making sure we had what we wanted in the three bags; some things were coming out, others going in; in between, we kept going back out to the cockpit, giving thumbs up to the hovering planes and throwing them kisses! We decided to carry Jason off in a seabag. I shoved him in to see if he fit. I zipped it up and then undid it to let him out. I served each of us a glass of wine and we toasted.

We turned on the radio to get the 11 a.m. news. They reported that a cargo vessel had diverted and was steaming toward us, expected to arrive in one to two hours. I packed my wallet, my manuscript and journals, my camera and lenses, eyeglasses, a few changes of clothing, the laptop computer and printer. Joy packed a few of her possessions. Now we waited for the ship. Where would they take us?

Around noon a large cargo vessel, looming on the horizon, steadily closed the distance between us.

"Joy. Look. There it is! It's here!" I had spotted the ship through one of our cabin's port lights.

"My God, look at that damn rust bucket!" Joy shouted, her voice sounding more animated than it had for days. The ship was a bluish-green with rust streaks running down her sides. She was massive.

"They don't want us to go up against that, do they? How? It will be the end of *Banshee*."

As Joy later told me, her emotions were so mixed about leaving the boat, our home, and yet elated at having been found. Yet something inside of her said *Banshee* would come back. It was that "light" in her premonition she had thought about as she lay down to sleep on the most horrible night.

Two or three hundred yards to windward, the ship stopped and they spoke to us on their loudspeaker. Could we swim to the ship? The *Maersk Sentosa* out of Singapore, on her way to Taiwan, stood by as we answered that we could not swim, not in 35 knot winds and 15 to 20 foot seas! Swimming would be suicidal. There was Joy's bum leg—and Jason.

Our response must have elicited from them the idea that someone might be injured. So they requested, "Raise your hands over your head if someone is injured."

We raised our hands, and they replied, "Negative."

That was frustrating. Both of us pointed to Joy's leg and then, with both hands, made a breaking motion.

"Yes. Someone is injured! Do you want to be taken off by helicopter?"

We held up a piece of paper on which we had written "yes" in large letters.

There followed a lengthy pause, perhaps as long as ten minutes. Probably they were communicating with rescue authorities on the radio. Finally, they told us we would have to board the ship because the rough seas made it impossible for the helicopter to lift us off our boat.

The ship's master, Captain Bob Fisher, thought it imprudent to bring the ship alongside the yacht as he feared it would smash us to bits. Now he had no choice but to come alongside. Slowly and carefully they eased the ship down onto us. I had been attempting to put Jason back into the seabag, but he resisted and scratched me across the forehead. The ship was getting close, and I needed to be on deck to take some lines.

I left the task to Joy. Jason knew he didn't want to go back into that bag. Several times he managed to get away and Joy could not chase him with her injured leg. Finally she grabbed him roughly and said, "It's your life, cat!"

When I came out on deck, I was shaking from watching the seas toss the two vessels. Five or six crew—Chinese, Indian and Malaysian—stood far above, gazing down at me. There was talk amongst them and one man tossed me a giant hawser, instructing me, in a heavily accented voice, to secure it to our beam. And then the two vessels collided. I could hear the paint scraping and cracking sounds from *Banshee's* hull. It could have been my arms or legs. I felt the pain as if it were my own.

Two more lines followed, one for the bow and one for the stern. The crunching sounds continued as the ship and yacht sawed up and down at different rates and slammed together. *Banshee's* going to break up, I thought with despair, but I dutifully attached the lines to our bow and stern. What I really wanted to do was push us off from this monster which was killing *Banshee*. With Joy safely off the boat, maybe I should sail her back myself. Was that foolish? I would be all right. I was torn. I wanted to go with Joy and Jason. If only I had a radio, then I could communicate, and sailing alone would be okay. I would know they were all right and Joy would know I was safe. My head was bursting with indecision.

By now Joy was in the cockpit with our three bags and Jason in the fourth. Our rescuers were dropping a line for our bags. Joy tied on Jason's bag first. As they lifted it, "Careful—that's a cat!" There was sudden surprise in their eyes and they almost threw the poor, bagged Jason back onto *Banshee*.

Joy yelled, "He won't hurt you. Just leave him in the bag."

As the other bags were being lifted off the deck, Joy was screaming in an agonized voice, fearing the worst for *Banshee*. And the crew above were shouting down, trying to comfort Joy, quiet her. Between the screams, the shouting, the action, the smashing and banging of the two vessels and my own thoughts racing through my head, it was bedlam for me. It was tortuous. With each slam of the vessels, Joy was wailing.

An Indian man with jet black hair flowing to his shoulders scurried down the Jacob's ladder and dropped onto our deck, timing his descent perfectly to avoid being crushed between the two wildly gyrating boats.

While talking in a soothing voice to Joy, he tied a line around her and supported her from below while those above adeptly and quickly pulled her safely up over the rail. He asked if I wished to be hauled up the same way, but I declined. I took the ladder, feeling that I wanted to be completely responsible myself for leaving *Banshee*. But I was torn. I strongly felt I should not be abandoning *Banshee*. Yet, I would take the ladder, placing my life in the hands of fate.

Everything was happening too fast. I could hardly comprehend that I was leaving *Banshee*. It was a nightmare. I had spent every day for almost six years aboard. *Banshee* was home. She was transportation from country to country. She was our passport to freedom, to a total way of life.

Joy was yelling her agony to the world. I was crying silently inside over my desertion, over *Banshee's* fate. I was certain I would never see my boat again. And I felt I didn't deserve to see her again because I was deserting. I was filled with dread, with sadness, and yet greatly relieved to be safe and to know Joy would soon have proper medical attention. Now I knew how afraid for her I had been these past few days.

Without even a chance to look back, I left *Banshee*. As soon as my feet touched the deck of the ship, several crew were escorting us below. They were trying to be comforting, saying the ship would tow *Banshee*. I knew and Joy knew that was impossible. A ship, moving at 18 knots or more, cannot tow a yacht. The yacht will go under.

Before leaving, Joy and I made a conscious decision not to pull the plug and sink *Banshee*. The radio beacon was still working. There was the slimmest chance that she could be salvaged. At least with her EPIRB, Sea Safety could issue a warning to shipping of her as a navigational hazard. The radio beacon would send a signal for days.

Amidst tears and yells of grief, Joy's final act aboard was to put in the hatch boards to keep the seas out and lock them with a brass padlock. Later she told me it was then she knew *Banshee* would be salvaged. That is why she used a brass padlock, because it is easy to saw through.

The crew took us to the hospital room and tucked us into beds piled high with a mound of warm blankets and a comforter. Jason, on Joy's bed, came out of his bag and Joy stroked him. Several crew stood by talking soothingly and changing places as someone else appeared. Such warmth and hospitality these seamen gave us.

In no time, a steaming cup of coffee sat on each of our bedside tables along with a sandwich. The steward, a short little man with clean shaven head, asked if Jason liked milk. Hot or cold? Joy assured him warm would be nice. Soon a huge bowl of warm milk was placed in front of Jason who was not too disturbed by his ordeal to drink his fill. Meanwhile the steward stood by to chat with us. He had the most amazing ability to shake his cheeks vigorously each time he nodded agreement.

In turn we were visited by the Chief Engineer and Captain Bob Fisher, who assured us he had been greatly concerned for his own ship in this horrendous storm. Captain Fisher said he thought we had weathered the situation well. He informed us they had to cut Banshee loose; they could not tow her. Then he said the helicopters would be there within about two hours. There was a problem. Australian authorities would not let us bring Jason with us.

"Why not?"

"Because we don't know where you're coming from, the cat cannot come into Australia."

"We've just come from Australia," we replied, with dismay, "where he served six months quarantine aboard our boat."

The captain left to speak with the officials again. It was only because of his persistence that the problem got ironed out and eventually resolved satisfactorily.

It came as a real shock that these authorities didn't know we had just embarked from Brisbane only ten days earlier, having filed a float plan with customs.

After about an hour and a half, I was told it was time for me to go on deck as the first Blackhawk helicopter was arriving. I was to take Jason with me, but some of the crew were still trying to fashion a container for him. I was rushed out without him, being told the helicopter could not wait. Joy was to depart in the second Blackhawk, coming with a medic to accompany her.

I followed three crew onto the deck. The ship rolled ponderously, spraying seas over the rail, wetting my legs and feet. Clad only in a pair of shorts, a t-shirt and a pair of running shoes, I was cold. We pushed our way against the wind, over the slippery deck to the bow. Hovering about 80 feet overhead, the Blackhawk created a strong draft that sprayed water everywhere and an ear-splitting noise that hurt my ears. A crewman from the helicopter, dressed in green fatigues, asked me, shouting over the noise, if I had ever been in a helicopter before. I answered no. He asked where the cat was. I yelled that he wasn't given to me. I saw our three bags on the deck in the spray, waiting. I asked about them. Can't take them, I was told. Quickly the crewman fastened me into a double harness with him. He showed me where to hang on and then we were rising in tandem straight up toward the whirling propeller. As they pulled me aboard, I looked down expecting to see the ship's deck but saw instead the marbled ocean below.

I was placed on a seat beside a pleasant young man who said, "If we have to ditch, I'm taking you with me. We'll go right out here," he said, pointing to the door over the wing. Soon they clapped a pair of earphones on my head with a small attached microphone and told me how to use it.

Now for the first time, I picked up from the conversation among the crew what the situation really was. The pilot said in standing by to pick up the crewman and me, the distance between the helicopter and the ship's deck kept fluctuating from 40 to 70 feet—one of the reasons this rescue was regarded as dangerous. This was a record flight for the Blackhawks. Never before had they flown this far, a round trip of 1400 kilometers or 870 miles! For this trip they had loaded on 1,000 pounds of extra fuel and still they were uncertain if it was enough to get us back to Rockhampton.

I admired these men who were risking their lives to save ours.

By coincidence the pilot, Mike Lehman, was a U.S. Army major on exchange duty from the 24th Infantry Regiment, Savannah, Georgia. It was a nice touch to hear a Yank accent as I was being rescued. There were four men on board and they talked sympathetically with me about our episode. They gave me two flight jackets to keep me warm, one to wear and one to wrap around my bare legs.

It was after 3 p.m. by the time I was airborne. Clouds had moved in since morning and, to avoid turbulence, the pilot kept elevating the craft above dark massing clouds up to a maximum of about 7,000 feet. Even at a lower altitude I noticed how difficult it was to look at the sea if searching for a boat. From the air, the sea flattened out and, with white foam and turbulence, it was a jumble. The angle of the late afternoon sun cast a gold and silver sheen over the water and reflected with a brightness that hurt my unprotected eyes. I was wishing for my sunglasses, but they, along with my clear glasses, were in the bags on the ship's deck.

The flight lasted just over three hours. As I sat back and relaxed for the first time in several days, I realized how weary I was. Perhaps there was some question as to whether the helicopter had enough fuel to make it back. *I* didn't worry about it. For once the responsibility was on someone else. That felt very good. I was bone weary from the weight of responsibility and stress of the recent days. I fully trusted these men to know their job. I could easily have drifted off to sleep except that I was enjoying the view, especially as we came to some coastal reefs and islands. In the fading light, the scene below was spectacular. The scattered reefs looked like a bejeweled necklace. I was also enjoying the banter between the men. As we got closer to land, they were discussing which restaurant they would go to that night, what they would eat and drink. At one point they reported to me that Jason and Joy were eating a Mars Bar. I asked if they got the bags on her helicopter. They said they didn't know. I was hoping they had. If not, I had no idea what we would do. We would have no clothes, no money, no credit cards, no glasses, no passports. Nothing but the clothes on our backs. Where would we stay that night? I thought Joy would probably be hospitalized, but there was nothing wrong with me. Where would I go?

It was after dark as we approached the Rockhampton airport. In the distance, the lights twinkled. I felt suddenly very relieved knowing my feet would soon touch terra firma. Finally we were landing. When the doors opened, we were told to remain in the craft until they had sprayed us. A familiar voice boomed out, "Hello, Jeannine. This is Dennis Young. Some people will do anything to get back into Australia!"

Dennis Young. Animal quarantine. We had met him upon our arrival in Australia. He shook my hand as I got out and introduced me to the customs official and the local constable. Without the flight jacket, I was shivering. The customs official said he was filling out the forms for immigration, too. I answered his questions and told him I had no passport with me. Hopefully Joy would bring it. They asked if I wanted to go to the hospital. I replied I would wait for Joy.

None too comfortingly, the constable confided to me that this was the week of Rockhampton's show, a county fair, and there wouldn't be any place to stay as motels would be full. Haven't the officials made any arrangements for us, I wondered to myself? I didn't say it but thought—without money I can't stay in a motel.

The customs official said the press had been made to stay outside. If I wished to speak with them I could, or not. I decided to do so. There was nothing else to do. The constable loaned me his jacket and, wearing this, I met the press with cameras flashing and several people jamming around asking questions simultaneously. I was lucky. Most of the press contingency had followed the ambulance when it drove away, thinking I was in it. They chased it all the way to the hospital before learning they were tailing an empty vehicle.

About an hour after I landed, Joy's helicopter arrived. They had carried her the entire way on a stretcher. For whatever reason, they did not give her a mike, so she missed the chance to speak with her rescuers. As soon as everyone had deplaned, Dennis Young took Jason out of a helmet bag and put him in a cage. Poor Jason. I went over and talked to him, but he was so distracted by all the people, the commotion and, no doubt, the noisy ride in the helicopter that he didn't even seem to know me.

I had already got Dennis Young to agree to taking Jason to Stu and Wendy's boat in Bundaberg, if they would have him. I didn't want him being sent all the way to Sydney and put in animal quarantine, which would be very expensive and unpleasant as he would be caged at all times and it would be too far away for us to visit him. Joy and I had discussed the possibility of Stu and Wendy taking Jason and we felt sure they would. Since they live on their boat, *Shalmar*, and have no phone, Dennis Young agreed to ask someone from Customs to go out to their boat and inquire.

It worked out. True friends that they are Stu and Wendy put their cat, Ginger, into a cattery and became Jason's foster parents for what proved to be more than a month.

It wasn't until Joy landed that I learned she and Jason almost stayed on the *Maersk Sentosa* and went to Taiwan! The ship's crew had made a makeshift splint for Joy's leg. They more or less carried her to the foredeck and were holding her up. When the helicopter crewman descended from the sky, Joy asked if he would take the cat. She couldn't hear his answer. She grabbed him and yelled again, "I'm going to Taiwan if you won't take the cat!" He said, loudly, "Lady, I'll take the cat!" She kissed him but wouldn't lie down on the stretcher as requested until Jason was ready to go.

"That cat's going to freak. We better transfer him to my helmet bag because I won't take him in that plastic contraption," the airman said indicating the makeshift container the crew of the *Maersk Sentosa* had fashioned for Jason. All at once five pairs of hands descended on Jason as the bucket was opened and he was popped into the helmet bag, zipped up and attached to a carabiner hook on the wire cable. Then Joy said she would lie down on the stretcher.

As the *Courier Mail* reported the incident on June 12, the cat nearly foiled the $2 million-dollar rescue. They reported Joy as saying, "I told them, Jason goes with us—or I don't go. He might just be a Kiwi cat from an animal shelter in Auckland, but we love him. He's like a child to us."

But unfortunately, Joy was not allowed to take any of our bags onto the helicopter. The reason was that they could not afford any additional weight since the flight was outside of their range even with the additional fuel. At least Joy was able to persuade them to let her dig our passports out of our bags and take them with her.

By the time we got to the Rockhampton Base Hospital, it was close to 8 p.m. Joy was hustled into an examination room only to wait and wait as no one appeared to examine her. We asked one male nurse if we could have some food. We'd had nothing since noon. He said the hospital kitchen closed at 8 and he had no hope of getting anything from them. He would look into it. Could we have coffee? They gave me a cup, but because Joy was going to be examined, they would not let her have any coffee.

No food came, but the male nurse, incongruously called "sister" here, made several phone calls, trying to find a place for me to stay overnight. He said Joy could remain in the hospital, but it would cost her $300 for one night! If I stayed, it would be an additional $300! I couldn't believe what I was hearing. We had just been rescued by extremely heroic measures, but now there was no place for us to stay? We had no money and no access to money. We expressed our shock and amazement to the nurse.

Finally the nurse called June Herrington, the director of the local Red Cross. She came to the hospital and I went out to talk with her. Once she heard about our difficulties, she invited both of us to stay at Red Cross House. It would cost us nothing. Also, she would take us to her son's motel for dinner.

After about an hour of waiting, a very overworked intern came to examine Joy's leg. As soon as he saw her, he inquired bruskly, "Who beat you up? Your old man?"

Joy said, "I am one of the women just rescued off a disabled yacht."

He responded, "I don't know anything about that. I only listen to the international news."

She was wheeled off to another area of the hospital for X-rays which showed that her leg was not fractured. After examining the X-rays the intern said, "Walk on your leg. No reason not to, it's just badly bruised!"

But one day of trying to walk on it proved this advice was wrong. When Joy's leg became more swollen and painful, she returned to the hospital the following day and saw another doctor. He wanted to know who had told her to walk on it. Walking on it started the bleeding again. He put her leg into an elastic support and admonished her to stay off the leg as much as possible and to walk only with crutches. It wasn't until we came to Mooloolaba almost a week later and saw a private physician that Joy learned what the damage was to her leg. When we turned over, she was thrown into the corner of the table. The impact, just below her knee, had ruptured her femoral vein. She must have lost, by the doctor's estimate, more than a quart of blood through internal bleeding—thus the pressure which caused so much pain.

After a lovely dinner at her son's restaurant, June dropped us off at Red Cross House, promising to return in the morning with food for our breakfast. Afterward she would let us pick out clothing from the Red Cross store, gratis. Good as her word, June returned early and cooked breakfast for us. We chose some clothes to be properly attired for a news conference we had agreed to beginning at 10 a.m.

Chapter 5

Living on the Edge

It must have been 11 p.m. when Joy and I finally closed the door to our room at Red Cross House. What a large, spacious room with an adjoining bathroom. Twin beds looked lost in this room that was almost big enough to encompass *Banshee*. As tired as we were, neither of us could resist taking a nice, long hot shower—the first in days. No doubt it took every minute I was in there to wash the salt from my pores.

Once the light was out and we had dropped onto our beds, we were exhausted, but sleep would not come. It was going to take a long time to unwind.

After a few minutes Joy spoke to me. "Jeannine, don't you feel strange?"

"You mean because there's no motion, no noise?"

"Yes, but something else too. There's too much room. I'm too far away from you. For years we've been living right beside each other. Do you mind if I move my mattress onto the floor beside your bed? I have to move the mattress onto the floor anyway because this bed's like a hammock."

"No, I don't mind. Come on over."

We must have talked for two more hours—even after all those days with little else to do but talk. But now, there were just so many unknowns from this day forward. Where does life go from here? Will we ever get our boat back? What do we do now? Questions of this type went on and on. And then, there was the knowledge that tomorrow the eyes of Australia would be on us. That was a bit disconcerting; we lead a very quiet, low-key life.

Daylight arrived all to soon and before we knew it, it was approaching 10 a.m. We walked across the street to the hospital and were led into a very large room arranged by the hospital for the news conference there. Soon we were seated on two chairs and within minutes the room filled to capacity, thronged with camcorders, TV cameras, still cameras, reporters and journalists.

Then the floodgates opened. It was an emotional time. Joy broke down and cried as she recalled details of our disaster. The reporters loved the drama. With the attention focused primarily on her, I could remain mostly quiet. When the official session ended, we were besieged by reporters wanting separate interviews and separate photo sessions.

During the conference, the hospital phone had been ringing incessantly for us. As soon as we came out, a stack of messages was dumped into our hands. When I could, I returned calls to our friends as well as numerous calls from people I didn't know and calls from reporters and TV stations seeking interviews. One of the calls was from Stu. He wanted to know how we were and said he and Wendy would be happy to take Jason for us. I told him we really didn't know how long Jason would have to be with them because at that time we didn't know what we were going to do.

Most of the day was taken up with interviews. Sometimes Joy was off on one interview while I was on another. By the time we returned to Red Cross House in the late afternoon, we found a stack of phone messages. Shirley, one of the ladies staying there, kindly answered the phone, which rang constantly, and took down numbers so we could return calls.

It was most disconcerting. Anytime the news came on TV, we saw ourselves and our pictures were plastered on the front pages of all the newspapers. We, who were used to leading a quiet life, could not even walk down the street without causing a sensation. Constantly we were besieged by throngs of people everywhere we went.

Upon returning in the evening to Red Cross House, we began returning phone calls, some to friends in New Zealand where our search-and-rescue had been followed almost as avidly as in Australia. Earlier that morning we had both tried calling our mothers. I failed to reach mine, but Joy was successful. Because her mother had not heard anything about our difficulties, she was surprised when she got a collect call from Joy.

"Mom," Joy said, "we're okay, but *Banshee's* gone."

"What do you mean?" said Joy's mother, not comprehending what Joy was saying.

"We were rescued. You've heard nothing? We were rescued after being dismasted in the Coral Sea."

"No, nothing here."

And then Joy described our saga in detail to her mother. Strangely, UPI carried nothing about the rescue in California papers, so our fears of upsetting our families were for naught.

I was not able to reach my mother that day. She called me the following morning and left a message for me. I called her back in Florida. She found out about our ordeal when a friend called her and asked if that wasn't her daughter mentioned in the local paper? My mother thought it was probably a notice or a review of my book. "No," her friend responded, "your daughter was rescued off the coast of Australia!"

At least we got our wish. Our mothers did not have to suffer any anxiety over our being lost at sea.

Many laudable aspects of human nature emerged. People from all over Australia called, offering free rooms, meals, sides of beef, clothing, a car on loan along with a mansion in an exclusive area for us to use for several days or weeks. Cat lovers wrote offering Jason a home—not realizing that quarantine would not allow them to take him—and commending us for not leaving him behind. Letters poured in, some with money; and packages of clothing arrived. And, most heartwarming of all, as we walked down the street, complete strangers came up to us, often hugging us, saying they were so glad we were alive. Many said they had prayed for us daily. These expressions of caring and concern restored my faith in the basic goodness of people and human nature. It was overwhelming.

At the first news conference, we met newsman John Ryan who had followed our story from the very beginning of the search and had video coverage from the search center as well. In the midst of all the commotion he got me aside and said he thought it was an absolute miracle that we were found. "Why?" I asked him. "Because," he claimed, "the search was conducted in the wrong area!" This information struck a resonant chord with what we had felt while adrift. He said he had the chart used by the flight center, showing the search area. I told him I would like to see it.

John Ryan and his wife, Lorraine, invited us to come and stay with them on their small farm a few kilometers from Rockhampton. After two days and two nights at Red Cross House, we decided to accept their invitation. This plan was good for several reasons. Conditions at Red Cross House were just getting out of hand. There were so many phone calls, June said they simply couldn't handle the volume. We hired an answering service where they also provided us with office space to work and a phone to use for making calls. Around this time, our dear friends Dave and Mary Francis borrowed a VW camper van and drove to Rockhampton from Mooloolaba to give us moral support and to help us deal with phone calls and mail. If we went to John's, they could bring the camper too, thus giving them a place to park at night. In this way the four of us could also be together in the evening to discuss things that we had to take care of. It was likewise helpful having John and Lorraine with us for their support and advice.

Before we moved to John's farm, a very important development came about. When we returned to Red Cross House toward evening on the second day we were in Rockhampton, Shirley placed another large pile of phone messages into our hands. Joy was reading through some while I read others. I came upon one which sent a wave of excitement through me.

"Joy, here's a message from a guy who says he wants to go get *Banshee!*"

"What? Who's that?"

"His name is Bedford. Bob Bedford. He wants you to call him."

"Give me that! Of course I'll call him. Where does he live?"

"Townsville. There's a number here. Says call collect."

"I will."

Joy called Bob, a fisherman, who said he wanted to bring *Banshee* back to us. Even more incredible, he didn't want a salvage fee! We couldn't believe it. Joy had said to him that he must be mad. He replied that he really wanted to do it because he and his deck hand, George Collins, had been sunk at sea in Bass Strait eight years before. When their 90-ton trawler was pooped and sank within about three minutes, they had to go to a liferaft. They just had time to get out a mayday on the radio and take to the raft. Somehow George was thrown out of the raft and Bob struggled frantically until finally he got him back in. Later a search craft flew very low over them and Bob fired a flare right in front of the plane. They were flying so low he could see the features of the men inside the plane, but the searchers did not see them or their flare!

It was July, winter, and they were in cold waters. Survival time, even in a raft was very limited—a matter of hours. One of their fishing mates knew the seriousness of their situation and, like many Australians, had little faith in the ability of the rescuers to find them. The mate took his ship to the area where he reckoned the men would be, and he found them. Bob said when he heard me describe the sound of the approaching sea that overturned us, it recalled his own horrible experience with shipwreck. Also, when he saw Joy's anguish on TV over the loss of her boat and home, he wanted to save *Banshee* for us. He only had two requests: we be there on the dock to meet him when he brought her in and, that afterward, we all go to the fishermen's pub and get "pissed."

Bob said they would not be able to leave immediately to search for *Banshee*. They were in the middle of a refit and the 63-foot *Saramoa* was on the hard. In fact, Bob had just purchased the *Saramoa* only several weeks before when he and George brought her north to Townsville in heavy weather. A wooden motor launch built in 1946 by the Australian Navy, *Saramoa* had spent most of her life as a light tender. Now Bob and George were rebuilding her for charter work and fishing. Bob said to keep in touch. Either he or his mother, Dot, would take our collect calls.

It was incredible. We simply couldn't believe someone would go out and take *Banshee* under tow and not want a salvage fee. We discussed this with Dave and Mary and with John and Lorraine. Still, we found it difficult to believe. Who was Bob Bedford? Was this just a joke? When we spoke to a Customs officer about the situation, he mentioned that it would not really be financially advantageous for anyone to bring in our boat for salvage. He pointed out that Australian law conflicted with international law. International law holds that the salvager has all rights to the vessel to sell at any price. Australian law, however, recognizes the yacht as an American vessel. First it would have to be imported, that is, the import fee—half of the vessel's value—would have to be paid to Australian customs before the salvager could claim ownership of the salvaged wreck.

Over the next few days there were several calls to Bob, and on several occasions Joy talked with Dot. When Dot told her that Mike Carney, a Toyota dealer in Townsville, had just donated $1800 to top up the fuel tanks, Joy had to conclude Bob's offer must be legitimate. Dot was reassuring. Bob and George fully intended to bring our boat back. But when were they going to go? We hoped it wouldn't be too long. We were concerned about *Banshee* being on her own too long. Since the electric bilge pump was not working, her bilge was probably filling up rather quickly. How long could she last out there?

A day or so after Bob called, Sea Safety in Canberra phoned us to report that they were picking up the EPIRB signal aboard *Banshee*! Each day we were hoping Bob would say they were ready to depart. Joy called him with the information that Sea Safety was picking up the signal and gave Bob *Banshee's* position. He was delighted to know that the EPIRB was working. That would make recovery much easier. But they still weren't ready to go.

During one phone call, Dot told Joy that Sea Safety refused to give Bob *Banshee's* position when he called them. I could not understand their refusal to give Bob the information. I called Sea Safety and asked why. They responded that they did not know who Bob Bedford was, even though it was big news in the papers. They were not sure whether or not he was a reputable person! I replied that he was the courageous and generous man who had volunteered to tow *Banshee* back for no salvage fee nor benefit to himself. At my request they continued to give the information to our answering service who then relayed it to Bob or his mother. The answering service called them regularly, usually twice a day, when the satellite passed over.

Five days after Joy and I had been rescued, Bob and George had the *Saramoa* refitted at last. Before the paint had even dried on the hull, she was relaunched and they departed Townsville, making for sea around midnight on June 15. The search for *Banshee* had begun.

While we were staying at John Ryan's farm, he gave me the chart he had promised, the one used by the flight rescue center, and showed us the videos he had made of conversations during the search for us. Some of this information interested us. The implications were that Sea Safety had made some questionable decisions in the search for us as well as the search for *Rockin' Robin*. Joy and I were quite concerned about the truth of the situation because, even though we had been found, the four *Rockin' Robin* men had not. The four-man crew of the *Rockin' Robin* were seen and photographed getting into a raft on June 8, being thrown out and finally, after great struggle, getting into the raft again. Aircraft stayed on station until 10:20 that night, but by morning they had lost the raft. The official search for the men had been called off on June 10, after only two more days. Unable to accept this decision and saying Sea Safety had bungled the search, the families of the four men were financing a private search.

We felt that it wasn't just a matter of nit-picking with Sea Safety, but that the discrepancies called for a serious probing into what had happened. If some procedures should be changed to assure more accuracy in future searches, then everything that had happened needed to be scrutinized. The chart from the flight search center designated the search area to be a considerable distance west of our position. Furthermore, according to John Ryan, the pilot flying the jet that located us the second time, said we were *outside* the search area. He claimed he found us only because he accidentally flew outside the grid. If true, then shouldn't Sea Safety be interested in what had gone wrong? It seemed we had been located by accident. Thank goodness we shot off the flare. This is how Brisbane observer Maurice Bathgate spotted us from the plane.

Joy and I were surprised that Sea Safety had never wanted to speak with us personally or to debrief us on our experience. They sent us a superficial form to fill out and return. Since it failed to cover many areas in depth and did not adequately address problem areas, Joy and I wrote about three pages of information we felt was critical to our experience.

With the new information I had been given by John Ryan, I decided to call the Federal Sea Safety Centre in Canberra and talk with them. I talked with Mike Taylor who immediately denied that we were outside the search area. Many assertions were to grow even more portentous as time passed.

Chapter 6

Welcome Back, Banshee

Within three or four days following our return to land, life
began to assume a fast pace along several paths simultaneously.
After about two days ashore, Jason had been moved to Stu and
Wendy's yacht, *Shalmar.* That was a great relief because we were
concerned about the trauma he had gone through and we knew his
separation from us was upsetting too. But at least he was with
people who loved him, who would lavish affection and attention on
him.

During our third day back, we learned that many of our friends
in Buddina at Lawrie's Marina, concerned about us and knowing
of our financial need, had started an appeal fund. Carol Moore,
who was to become something of a "personal minder" to us, headed
up the appeal, even going on TV to publicize the effort. She
immediately sent funds to us and clothing, for which we felt great
gratitude. Many of the contributors were unknown to us; others
were old friends with whom we'd been sailing for some time. The
response proved to us what a strong *esprit de corps* exists among
cruisers.

Of course word traveled quickly that the *Saramoa* had left on
her mercy mission and hopes were running high that with a lot of
luck *Banshee* would be saved. People who knew us realized she
was not just a boat to us but a way of life, a way to pursue our
dreams of visiting remote areas of the world, becoming acquainted
with people of various ethnic and cultural backgrounds.

Because we manage our cruising on very limited funds, *Banshee* was not insured. We couldn't afford to go cruising if we had
insurance. What many non-sailors don't know is that in the States
it is not easy to obtain insurance when cruising. We looked into it
before leaving California and were told we would not be eligible
unless there were four people on board! There is not room for four
people to cruise on *Banshee.*

Often we encounter the erroneous attitude that everyone who owns a yacht is wealthy, especially those making long distance voyages. Such people view us as leading a life of the idle rich, having no concept that we expend hours of effort maintaining our boat. We do almost everything ourselves because it is too expensive to pay someone to do maintenance and also because we want things done correctly. Additionally, much of the time we visit remote areas where there is no one knowledgeable about repairing yachts and their equipment. Joy and I have an expression that illustrates our attitude in this respect—"There are no plumbers at sea." Our lives depend on our being able to make all kinds of repairs—even at sea.

Periodically we stop in our travels to work. Our last work stop was in New Zealand for one and a half years where Joy taught high school science and I finished writing a book.

As in any lifestyle, there are trade-offs. We have no home, save *Banshee*, no property to return to. We go for several years not seeing close friends or family in the States, but we make friends everywhere we go and have been "adopted" by several families. Most of the time we have no 9-to-5 jobs and never have mortgages or other attendant expenses typical of land-based people. We have exchanged the comfort and security of routine life with abundant luxuries for an ever-changing montage of landscapes, languages, friends, foods; a steady, non-rocking house and garden for a compact living area that tilts and sometimes wildly throws us around. We live by the sun, wind, stars and have become creatures more adapted to living close to nature—subject to its heat, cold, and storms—than we are to the ease of central heating, air conditioning and convenience of mall shopping. We have swapped the sedate, the sedentary routine for adventure. No doubt there are those envious of our relative freedom, our apparent carefree lifestyle, or some snobs who think of us as gypsies—the very scum of the earth! Yet there are people who admire anyone with enough independence and imagination to sever ties with civilization and embark on a life of unknown adventure. Such persons wisely comprehend that most of us have some corner of the brain that needs or relishes even the vicarious experience of chasing dreams and following their wanderlust to the ends of the world.

As some wag long ago said, "Traveling is broadening." We could add to that, "Traveling by yacht is the most expensive way to travel fourth class, but it gets you to the hearts of others free enough to embrace the stranger from a strange land who sails in over the horizon."

At Lawrie's Marina in Buddina, friends were planning a homecoming party for us. John Ryan offered to drive us down from Rockhampton, suggesting that we stop overnight in Bundaberg. If we did, it would give him a chance to film a reunion of us with Jason, which he thought would make a good TV human interest story.

On June 16 we drove with John while Dave and Mary followed in the VW van. They too would stay overnight in Bundaberg before returning to Buddina. The first friends we saw in Bundaberg were Pat and Allan from *Smokey Bear* who had loaned Dave and Mary their van. Pat and Allan were tied up at the marina. They greeted us with hugs and excited talk. Once we settled down on their boat with other friends, we noticed that Pat and Allan were exchanging secretive glances and whispers. They started passing out glasses.

With a big smile and hearty laugh, Allan brought a bottle of champagne into the cockpit and said, "I have a toast—*Banshee* has been sighted!"

What happened was that John Salter, chief of North Queensland Emergency Response Group, gave his pilots permission, after they had begged him, to divert 100 miles from their search for the *Rockin' Robin* crew to look for *Banshee*. They had sighted her and said she looked good! What reassuring news. Both of us had been tormented by horrible thoughts and nightmares about *Banshee* out there on her own.

A bit later, after we had talked excitedly about the return of *Banshee*—something we hardly dared to hope for—Allan took us by dinghy to *Shalmar* moored in the middle of the river.

How good to see Wendy and Stu again—and Jason. After more hugs we launched into a lengthy session of questions and answers with Stu and Wendy who told us how distressed they had been knowing of our problems at sea. Jason's greeting was far more offhanded, rather aloof. Not that he didn't know us. He did, but I guess this indifference was his way of expressing his anger that we had deserted him. But it was short lived. That night he crawled into my bunk, started purring and spent the night curled up against my legs.

On Sunday morning when John brought his video camera over, Jason was back to being himself. He struck beautiful poses and hammed it up just as if he knew what he was doing. But, when we left, Wendy said he became despondent. For days afterwards, Jason sat on deck just staring in the direction we had gone. For some time he was inconsolable and indifferent to them or their attention.

Before leaving Bundaberg, we had a very brief chat and reunion with Brian and Joan off *Cape Louisa*. Joan told us that when she heard a yacht was in trouble, she knew it was us (and she didn't even know we had set sail, and we had not seen them for over two years). Brian, who is used to Joan's psychic perceptions, just accepted her pronouncement and said it came as no surprise when they later heard our names on the news. Joan said she told Brian not to worry because she *knew* we would be rescued.

We barely got out of the car at Lawrie's Marina before throngs of people surrounded us, all talking, laughing, hugging and squeezing us at the same time. Everyone was telling us how awful they had felt when they heard about our dismasting. Some had given up hope, but others never gave up. They thought we would stay with *Banshee* and survive. Some even called Sea Safety to assure them we were competent sailors and knew what to do. They also told how they cheered when hearing we had been found, how they had prayed for us. Ron on *Delirium* said he was reading my book when he first heard about our disaster. After that he couldn't read it anymore as it upset him too much. When he heard we had been picked up, he started reading it again.

For the next couple of days we stayed with Helen and Peter Turton who gave us a room in their home and a place to store some of our newly acquired clothing. They had assured us we would be welcome upon our return from Townsville.

By now we had had a full week of the media who habitually turned up wherever we were. Probably we tended to stay in the news day-to-day because the search for the *Rockin' Robin* men continued. Our success story was used to augment everyone's fervent hopes for finding the men. Sea Safety's decision to abandon the search for the men on the day we were rescued understandably outraged the families of the missing men. Convinced that 62-year-old Grant Wiltshire and his 34-year-old son, Robert, and his friends, Jeffery Smith and Andrew Young, both 34, were still alive, drifting in the liferaft dropped to them, the families paid for a private search at the rate of $25,000 per day!

It was, in fact, a bit of a sore spot with some Australians that two Americans had been rescued while four Australians had been lost. Several letters to the editor suggested that people who go to sea in small boats are fools, which, of course, paved the way for asking why should they be rescued at public expense? Occasionally the press referred to us as the "million dollar women" because the rescue—according to the media—had cost $2.4 million dollars. Jason was dubbed the "$14 million-dollar cat", the price of one Blackhawk helicopter like the one that rescued us.

The stated high cost of search-and-rescue generated a flap about the use of public funds to save persons in distress at sea. Worse yet, some individuals turned it into an ugly chauvinistic issue, asserting that Australian search-and-rescue be used only for Australians! Fortunately, this latter extreme view attracted few supporters, but the argument against using public funds for sea rescue never was satisfactorily countered. Why didn't someone point out that boaters in Australia pay high taxes on all boating gear and equipment they buy, thus contributing in a very substantial way to sea search-and-rescue? Perhaps the most persuasive counter argument is: how does the use of taxes to save someone in trouble at sea differ from the use of taxes in a national healthcare system to pay for kidney transplants, heart bypasses and numerous kinds of lifesaving medical procedures? Not only that, since the military routinely fly mock missions and rescues, much of this cost exists with or without a real search. So the cost to taxpayers of search-and-rescue, as presented by the media, was in many respects very misleading.

As one person said to me, "What these critics don't stop to think about is that anyone who buys a boat and goes to sea has to have so much more on the ball than the complainer who does nothing more imaginative than staying glued to the soaps."

To me, perhaps the most annoying criticisms were those that accused people going to sea as being irresponsible and stupid. No doubt some are, but I believe the majority are knowledgeable and exercise prudence.

On Monday we got word that Bob Bedford and George Collins had *Banshee* in tow!

On Tuesday morning we were on the road again with John Ryan, this time going north on the long drive to Townsville to meet the *Saramoa*. We had kept in contact with Dot Bedford, who usually spoke with Bob by radio each night. From her we learned that the men were having a tough time with 30-knot winds and high seas. When they boarded *Banshee,* she was knee deep in water. That was bad news. Where was the water coming in? Their first thought was that the head was leaking. They shut off the head valve, bailed the vessel dry and thought their problems were over, only to find that she was still taking on water at a pretty good rate. This is when George realized to keep *Banshee* afloat he would need to stay on board to bail and pump. This action caused many heartstopping moments.

Then there was another heartstopping period. Just about the time they were coming through the reef, they were struck by gale force winds. Bob knew he was running low on diesel fuel and in the rough seas *Saramoa* was rolling so furiously he couldn't read his fuel gauge. Dot was very concerned. She said if Bob ran out of fuel, it would take $2,000 to buy more fuel to be delivered to him by a mate, and Bob didn't have the money. We told her we didn't know how we could raise $2,000, but we would try our best. It could mean the difference between having *Banshee* and losing her!

For a while it seemed touch and go, as if on the final leg of the tow they might lose *Banshee* in this terrible blow. What if they couldn't control her in the storm or if she took on too much water? She might sink. Fortunately, conditions calmed and the fuel held out.

Dot Bedford had invited us to stay in their home. Around dusk on Wednesday evening we arrived at the Bedford residence and were welcomed by Helen, Bob's lady, and Dot.

Also present was Kerry Brown, the young woman whose answering service we had hired in Rockhampton. Having phoned Sea Safety twice each day to get *Banshee's* position that was picked up by satellite, and then called Dot with the information so she could relay the position to Bob, Kerry had become so involved in *Banshee's* rescue, she asked if she could be there too. Dot had rooms and beds ready for all of us, including John Ryan.

Bob had advised Dot that they would probably be coming in around 5 a.m. Thursday, June 23. All of us were up at 4 a.m., awaiting Bob's call. When 6 then 7 came, and still no word from Bob, all of us were thinking something terrible must have happened. Joy and I were feeling very apprehensive. Finally a fierce roar pierced the silence as a motorcycle sped up the driveway. Graham Bedford, Bob's father, rushed in—"What's wrong with the phone? Bob's been calling for about two hours!" The phone was unplugged!

Instantly we all hurried outside, climbed into two vehicles and lurched off for the marina. Graham was waiting at the dock with a large tender, big enough to take all of us out into the bay where the *Saramoa* was anchored.

I knew by Joy's tearful face that she was finally letting down her guard and releasing some of the extreme pressure and excitement that had been building over the past week. Knowing how emotional Joy was, Dot reached over and held her hand the whole way. My heart was racing as we flew across the lumpy water, spray splashing my face. Outside the breakwater the *Saramoa* lay, rolling languidly in the swell. Gradually the far side of *Saramoa* came into view. There lay *Banshee* securely tied to her, looking almost the way she did when we left her. My heart was hammering so fast I thought my chest would burst. Even now, seeing her, I could hardly believe it.

Joy said to Graham, "Let me touch her," and he brought the tender closer so she could caress *Banshee*. Joy and I were crying and still wiping tears from our eyes as we boarded *Saramoa*, helped aboard by burly Bob. Each of us clutched him in an ebullient bear hug and then clamped our arms around George, brushing against his face, bristly with whiskers.

I have never warmed so quickly to two complete strangers. They didn't feel like strangers at all. There was an immediate rapport amongst us, stemming from our shared bond of the sea. They were exactly as I had pictured them, honed to unselfconscious honesty by the sea, and hard as granite, two beefy, strong seamen, toughened by sea, storm, shipwreck, survival, but still harboring soft hearts.

For the moment we could only look at Banshee, not board her. Customs had told us to stay clear of her until they came out to inspect. Fortunately it was a while before the media hounds could find transportation out to *Saramoa*, so momentarily Bob and George had a chance to relate some of their electrifying saga.

Accomplished seamen, they had come within a mile of *Banshee* going on their estimate of where they would rendezvous. Just after 6 a.m. out of the half light emerged *Banshee*. storm tossed, almost an apparition lumbering over the turbulent seas, surrounded by the mysterious air of an abandoned vessel. One side of her looked undamaged, but her jagged stump of mast told more than a small part of her recent tragedy. She had that silent, empty look of a deserted boat—forlorn, as if perhaps she was mourning those whose laughter once resounded in her cabin. Bob and George could sense those secrets lurking within seeping out and enveloping her external visage. She was low in the bow and looking like she could go down within a matter of hours to her watery grave.

Realizing there was no time to linger over vague thoughts and feelings, George, undaunted by 30-knot winds and very rough seas, jumped over the side and swam with a towline to her. His former experience as a Navy diver was standing him in good stead now. With his strong arms, he pulled himself up onto *Banshee's* deck without too much trouble. Once aboard, he secured the towline to the mast. George knew he needed to go below and check things out. He had no tools with him, but the brass lock was no deterrent. With one massive hand, he grasped the lock and yanked until the latch, bedded in fiberglass, gave way.

For a week *Banshee* had been on her own with no one to pump her bilge. Below, George sloshed around in knee-deep water. Desperately he tore up the floor boards, searching for the hand pump we had told him was there. But it didn't work. The pump must be clogged with debris and the water was still coming in. He found a saucepan in the cupboard and began bailing furiously. It was a horrendous, tiresome job. George said that for every 20 seconds he bailed, it took two seconds to fill up again. Eventually he and Bob were able to take one of our small electric pumps and one of theirs and, using them in tandem, pump the water from the inside out into the cockpit until she was pumped dry.

But, unfortunately, the next morning, she had filled again. It now became obvious that one man had to stay aboard her to continue bailing and pumping. George stayed for three days and nights without sleep, keeping vigil, bailing. Only after he ascertained the head was not leaking did he discover there was a separation of the hull deck joint, extending from her port bow to her beam. Additionally there were three holes in the deck at the bow where the bow pulpit and the bow roller had been lifted up by pressures exerted when *Banshee* collided with the rescue ship. All of the major hull damage, in fact, occurred when we went alongside the ship. Between the heavy seas and the bow wave when she was under tow, water was pouring in through these openings.

Even with a towline on, the men were not home free. They had also incurred considerable damage sustained when falling off some huge seas which had opened up some of *Saramoa's* seams. Now she too was taking on water, but at least her bilge pumps weren't plugged. One of the worst things to happen was that their autopilot quit, enslaving Bob to the wheel with no relief because George was aboard *Banshee*.

To make matters worse, *Banshee* didn't behave well under tow. Instead of tracking in a straight line, she slewed from side to side as sailboats do, but at least this motion meant she wouldn't snap the towline, which stretched in diameter to a quarter of its original size!

Miraculously the fuel held out, just, allowing them to come into the outside harbor at Townsville. Then the fuel line went dry. Bob dropped his anchor right there and pulled *Banshee* alongside.

Much of this story we heard in *Saramoa's* main saloon around the table eating a substantial breakfast prepared by Kerry.

Perhaps 45 minutes after us, the media began arriving and finally, Customs. The next two or three hours were chaos. All Joy and I wanted to do was get aboard and start removing electronic equipment so we could send it some place for quick servicing. With saltwater damage, time was of the essence. But the media were there, underfoot, pestering, insistent. They wanted to see the inside, they wanted interviews, photographs. It went on and on, dozens of reporters milling around, pressing in.

After a couple of hours Bob became impatient. "Let's go to the pub!" he shouted. But latecomers with tape recorders, pads and cameras kept streaming on and over the two boats. We couldn't get rid of them. Joy and I had been through almost two weeks of publicity which had been wearing. Bob and George had been through a physically and emotionally demanding experience at sea, days without sleep. They needed to escape and unwind. They don't drink at sea, but when they return, the first stop is the fishermen's pub!

Finally we banished the press. The guys took off straight for the pub and accompanying them was Mike Carney, our generous benefactor who had contributed fuel for the recovery operation. Before we could go, Joy and I wanted to get our electronic gear packaged and delivered to the bus station so it could go to Mooloolaba and be worked on. Carol would pick it up at the bus station and drive it to the technician.

I have heard about cathartic releases before, but I never witnessed anything so dramatic as the one at the pub. By the time Joy and I arrived, the discharge of pent-up emotions was progressing in a vivid manner. One of the forms it took was aggressive bantering between Bob and George who squared off like mortal enemies, threatening to punch each other out, their physical antics supported by a thunderous roar of incessant profanities. It was Australian mateship raised to its ultimate.

Yet private conversations with each man saw the bravado evaporate, replaced by emotions of caring and real concern for each other. With tears in his eyes, invincible Bob said to me, "I was afraid George was going to die. I thought I would lose him." They have been going to sea together for 12 years.

Both men argued tenaciously that we should change the name of the boat because they think *Banshee* is a name bringing bad luck. George said to me, "That boat tried to kill me! I heard voices on her, but I couldn't understand what they were saying!"

"Yes," I responded. "Did it sound like a radio that wasn't tuned and the volume too low?"

"Yes, that's it!"

"George, I always hear that sound in bad weather, but Joy never hears it."

"You know what I heard! That's it exactly!"

Hearing George describe what I've heard many times gave me an eerie feeling.

Yet, it seems to me the name has brought us good luck. We survived and *Banshee* survived.

And there was another inexplicable, ominous occurrence in addition to Joy's unrelenting premonitions. Bob's brother-in-law was out on an army maneuver during the time we were lost at sea. He knew nothing of our plight, but one night he dreamed about *Saramoa*. She was towing a yacht!

Thursday night *Banshee* and *Saramoa* remained in tandem in the outer harbor as their crews extended the homecoming celebration into the night. Early Friday morning we all dinghied out to the two crafts to bring them into the marina. While still at sea, Bob had got *Banshee's* engine going after finding it had an air lock. We drove her into the slip next to *Saramoa* under her own power.

Once tied up in the slip, Joy and I had to deal with the total devastation that awaited us below. It was a heartbreaking mess. Everything was soggy, smelly, moldy—many things waterlogged, ruined. I felt depressed and hardly knew where to begin. Moving about on crutches with great difficulty, Joy was unable to do much. Her incapacity to work rendered her cranky and bossy. And her bad temper only added to my depression. If it hadn't been for two very kind people, I might still be there uncertain where to begin. Ron and Lila Jones and their little four-year-old daughter, Margaret, walked down the dock toward me and began speaking. They were off the New Zealand yacht *Pacific Express* and they wanted to know if they could help us. Joy heard us talking outside on the deck and she hobbled out to join in. She had heard their offer to help and said, "We can't afford to pay you anything."

Ron and Lila both responded instantly, "We don't want any money. We just want to help you."

"Oh, that would be lovely. How kind!" I felt like crying. Work they did. They took charge because I wasn't able to think constructively. Never have I seen two people work so industriously. Everything had to come out of the boat and be stored until we could get the inside hosed down and dried out. All our charts were wet—several thousand dollars worth—and I knew they had to be opened up to dry thoroughly if we were going to save them. I spoke with Coral, the marina manager, to inquire if they had a room where I could spread out the charts. She let me use three large, almost empty rooms. Come Monday, I could have access to only one of them. That was fine. The only hitch was that the offices were upstairs, which made the task of carrying all the charts considerable.

I came back to the boat after several hours of chart spreading to learn that someone in the marina had given us their van to use as storage. This too was a momentous production as it meant moving everything, two or three boxes at a time, in a cart from the far end of the dock up to the parking lot. But Ron and Lila worked with a will. By now they had tied some of our lines between piles so they could dry out all our cushions. These had been stripped of their ruined upholstery, the foam thoroughly washed in fresh water and then hung up. Lots of people came by to stare and look, even to take pictures. Some other yachties offered to help too. These people will have our eternal gratitude for their efforts and caring.

Among the onlookers was a youngish man, brash and swaggering in the manner of some hot shot racers who see themselves as God's gift to the yacht club set. Three or four of us had been standing beside *Banshee* talking for a few moments when the braggart looked directly at Ron and said, "Well, mate, tell me what happened out there."

Ron, who is a gentle, soft-spoken man, looked rather pained and glanced at me with an empathetic look. After all the publicity, no one in Australia could have been ignorant of the fact that there were two women aboard *Banshee*, no men. I looked the posturing Adonis directly in the eye and said, "Why are you asking him? He wasn't there!" It was a blow that hit him where it hurt and left him speechless.

The *Silver Cloud* crew, Lou and Liz, both came by and helped on several occasions. On our second day of cleaning, Brian and Jill Robinson, members of the Coastal Cruising Club, came by to chat. They wanted to know about our ordeal in detail so they could write it up for *The Mainsheet,* the Official Bulletin of the Coastal Cruising Club.

Brian and a crew of helpers removed the mast stump. Jill and Brian hauled off four bags of sodden bedding and clothing to the laundry, which they paid for, and invited us out for a lovely dinner under the stars at an old Townsville Pub. They also took my electronic keyboard back to Sydney with them to check it out.

One of our biggest problems was finding enough boxes to pack everything. But soon this problem had a solution, as did our transportation to and from the marina to the Bedford home. One day Kevin and Ailsa McMahon stopped by to chat. They wanted to meet us and find out if they could help us in some way. Ailsa saw a stack of dirty laundry and offered to take it home and wash it. Their home was only several blocks from the Bedfords, so Kevin offered to be our chauffeur morning and evening. A retired railway employee, Kevin loved to tease us about how much his transportation bill would amount to.

On one of these days Ann on *Lion Wing* washed some of our things, and her husband, Beau, removed all the fittings from the mast stump.

After about four days of work, Ron and Lila left the marina. Everyone else had gone too because people were making passages up the coast. Townsville was just a stopping off place for a night or two. We were on our own again, but certainly not out of jobs. All our electric power tools—drill motor, sander, and jigsaw—had taken a saltwater bath as had all our hand tools. We washed everything thoroughly in fresh water and then I soaked all the hand tools in diesel fuel. They remained for three or four weeks with the residue of diesel before Joy was able to clean them. The diesel stopped the rusting and oxalic acid removed the rust, and the acid, in turn, was cleaned off with detergent and water. Most of the tools looked like new after this treatment, but the power tools, unfortunately, were ruined. I was still drying charts and trying to dry books and music. Michael, an eight-year-old New Zealand lad, spent a lot of time spreading out books over the docks and opening them up so the wind and sun could dry them. Sadly most of our better books, the glossy, color-illustrated ones did not survive.

One day, about the time we had started loading everything back onto *Banshee*, a boat named *Banjo* pulled into a nearby slip. While talking with them, we learned that Aussies Brian and Judy were also members of the Seven Seas Cruising Association, as are we. They pitched in and made short work of one hard job. After that, Judy was always feeding us, as had Lila, because there was only one fast food place convenient to the marina. Most of our evening meals were with the Bedfords, who hosted us for the eleven days we were in Townsville. Wanting to help them out as much as we could, we gave them much of our canned food and some money to offset the cost of our meals with them and our phone calls.

Those eleven days were some very emotional times for us. We also learned, much to our dismay, that the Bedfords were in a financial crunch at the time. Bob had just invested every penny he had in *Saramoa* and Graham too had recently sunk his money into his business. This family, despite their own hardships and struggles, had opened their arms to us.

During this time we were trying to find someone who would truck *Banshee* south to Lawrie's Marina. Being a trip of around 800 miles, it was an expensive proposition, but staying in Townsville would have been prohibitively costly, parts would have to be brought in from Brisbane, and we had no place to live for the eight months or longer it would take to rebuild *Banshee*. Whereas in Buddina, we had been offered accommodations, and Keith Lawrie had offered us free hardstand in his boatyard. Finally Carol found Bob Bobbermein who gave us a good rate to truck *Banshee* south.

119

We promised him publicity—which he got in Townsville, Rockhampton and Buddina.

Meanwhile the *Rockin' Robin* search, financed by the families and public donations, was continuing. Graham and Bob Bedford both felt confident the crew were still alive in the raft. Our rescue, the recovery of *Banshee,* and the survival of a French woman who washed up in a raft on the shores of Papua, New Guinea, were spreading renewed confidence that the four men were alive. Graham got all the weather maps from the Met Bureau from the time the men left their yacht up to the present, and then set to work plotting their drift based on wind velocity and direction and currents. The Bedfords contacted the families and explained they thought they could find the raft. But they needed fuel to embark on this search. This time they needed not only full tanks, but many extra gallons stored on deck in barrels.

Once again the *Saramoa* was on the hardstand being repaired for her next mission. Finally fuel was donated and enough food to carry them through for a 21-day expedition. Joining Bob, Graham, George and one of their friends were David Issacs, friend of the Wiltshires, and Mike Wood, Grant Wiltshire's son-in-law. Around midnight on June 28 we went down to the wharf in Townsville to see the crew off and wish them well.

On July 2 *Banshee* came out of the water and waited overnight in a cradle until Bob Bobbermein pulled up with his truck. In just over three hours *Banshee* was loaded on the truck, secured and ready for the road.

That night Joy and I left Townsville on the bus. We arrived in Rockhampton early the next morning and were met by John Ryan who drove us to the airstrip where searchers were preparing to fly out on another attempt to locate the raft with the *Rockin' Robin* crew. David Issacs and Mike Wood, who had left *Saramoa* in Rockhampton, were going in the plane as observers. The *Saramoa* crew thought they had spotted something and the plane would fly over to check it out. The air crew, who planned to get an early start, were held up waiting for the arrival of a Global Positioning System (GPS). GPS, developed by the American Department of Defense, is the latest in satellite navigation. When completed, it will consist of 24 satellites that provide 24-hour, three-dimensional navigational coverage. To date there are 11 satellites in place. We learned from the pilot that it is difficult to position objects at sea with accuracy from a plane. For this reason they needed the GPS before leaving on this search, as their navigation had to be spot on.

For the first time I talked with David and Mike about their own experiences in the same storm we had survived. They were on *Winnifred*, a home-built Roberts 52 (but built to 54 feet) and had set sail at the same time as *Rockin' Robin* as a companion boat. After leaving Newcastle bound for Noumea, the two boats ran into bad weather. *Winnifred* sought refuge in Port Stephens, while *Rockin' Robin* went on to Seal Rocks *before* turning back to Port Stephens. Two days later, when the weather had settled, both yachts set out once more. *Winnifred* went directly to Middleton Reef, thinking their friends on *Rockin' Robin* were right behind. Because of faulty radio equipment aboard the larger boat, they were not able to keep a radio schedule with *Rockin' Robin* and did not know that they had pulled into Coffs Harbour to deal with an alternator problem. *Winnifred* continued on toward Noumea and was caught in the cyclone. Several of their ports were bashed in by heavy seas, but with six crew, they were able to have some crew hold pillows and blankets over the open ports while others made wood port covers which they secured by through bolting. Though damaged, they made Noumea and when they heard of *Rockin' Robin's* tragedy, Mike and David returned to Australia to lend support and assistance.

Another unfortunate boat caught in the unseasonal storm was *My Affair*, a 36-foot catamaran heading for Noumea. Thirty-one-year-old John Blahuta, sailing with three male crew, described it as "the worst weather I've ever experienced." They left Brisbane on June 3 and were badly damaged three days later. On the morning of June 8, when the *Rockin' Robin* crew had taken to a liferaft, *My Affair* was struck by a big wave which filled the boat with water, dislodging and accidentally inflating their liferaft so that it became jammed in the cockpit. But their problems had really started the previous afternoon when in 45-knot winds and

20- to 25-foot seas, their windows were smashed in and a crewman suffered a broken collarbone.

Only 20 miles from *Rockin' Robin,* they heard frantic mayday calls from the doomed sloop. Blahuta also heard about our plight and these problems only added to his own worries. Because of his difficulties, he was unable to render assistance to *Rockin' Robin.* Blahuta and his crew turned back for Australia, hoping to make Fraser Island, but they were blown off course and ended up at Gladstone. *My Affair* made it, but Blahuta said she was a real mess.

Still another vessel's destiny put her into this same severe low. Yachtsman Philip Nitschke, 32, of Darwin, and his companion, Marlies Blatz, 32, of Sydney, had left Sydney bound for Darwin two weeks before the storm. Taking shelter from bad weather and huge seas at Byron Bay, they developed a serious problem. The anchor rope became tangled with the propeller. With deteriorating weather, they had no choice but to sail to Cook Island. When they struck huge seas, they called for urgent assistance late Thursday, June 7. The water police boat and Point Danger Air Sea Rescue boats towed the yacht to the protected waters off Rainbow Bay. But rough conditions that night prevented them from sleeping. In the morning Nitschke tried diving under the boat to free the prop, but it was too rough for him to complete the job. At this point, feeling their lives were endangered, they asked to be taken off their yacht, *Squizz,* and they were.

Ironically it was the smallest boat, *Pom Pom,* a Herreschoff 28, that fared the best in this storm. Barry and Margaret, with whom we had a lengthy conversation eight months after the storm, were situated about 30 miles north of us. Their worst problem was water coming into their boat because of the bashing seas. They stayed hove to and battened down for several days until conditions settled down enough to get underway again. Their experience and the beating they took was bad enough that they aborted their planned voyage to the Solomons and sailed back to Townsville.

It came as no surprise to me when I read that Bundaberg Air Sea Rescue workers described conditions during this low as "worse than the last cyclone."

Chapter 7

Aftermath

Life between June 10 and the end of July swooped along in schizophrenic waves as our destiny took sharp and steep turns. To live for a week fearing our boat would sink to the bottom and become an artificial reef for sea life was a dreadful experience. What would we do without Ba*nshee*? Go back to the States and earn enough money to buy another boat and start over? Change strides and do something entirely different? We didn't have any answers. We had to wait and see.

Then, suddenly, our fortune changed. Our future was charted. We had a boat to rebuild. *Banshee* was back, and from the exterior, not looking too bad—considering what she had endured. Even so, the damage was extensive—more than cosmetic—and affected just about every system and area of the boat. The interior suffered enormous water damage. The upholstery was ruined and all painted and varnished surfaces needed redoing. The tile behind the fireplace had shaken loose and many pieces dropped off. Smeared throughout the interior was a concoction of rust, diesel oil, bilge water and rotten food.

After all the punishment from the sea and from going up against the cargo vessel, every chainplate had to be carefully inspected to ascertain its soundness. To do so meant removing interior teak planks forward and in the main cabin so we could inspect them.

Outside too the boat was a shambles. All the stainless steel stanchions were bent, as were many of the stanchion bases, as well as the bow and stern pulpits. The tremendous force of the seas had twisted one-inch stainless steel tubing! Virtually everything had to be removed from the deck. A gargantuan task. The hull, newly painted just before we left Australia, was badly scraped, gouged and nicked. It would need fiberglass repair, sanding and repainting. To do a good job of it, the entire boat would need repainting. Robert Forbes, the painter who had sprayed the hull before we left, offered to redo it at no cost for his labor. The names on both bows had to be repainted, but the stern just needed touching up.

The lifelines, also replaced just prior to leaving Australia, were severely damaged. Inspection of the rudder showed it to be undamaged, but the rudder stops were bent from the wild thrashing of the rudder. They would need to be removed, straightened and galvanized before they could be refitted. Replacing the mast and rigging meant not only those items themselves, but all the electrical wires in the mast, navigation lights, steaming light, deck light and radar reflector. And, of course, we had to have two new sails built to replace the two we had lost. All our halyards and sheets were gone. The amount of work was overwhelming—the cost staggering.

Once again, we had to remove all the contents from the boat when she was back in Buddina sitting in a cradle. Boat gear, tools, electronics, books, musical instruments, clothing, food and so on went to various places, some to homes of friends, some to a storage shed we rented. A few items went to the 25-foot power boat Jeff Brown kindly loaned us to live on while we made *Banshee* liveable. Again Carol Moore had been looking out for us. Long before our return to Lawrie's Marina, she was finding a place for us to live. She found Jeff and made the arrangements.

For almost a month we'd been living from pillar to post, staying with friends in their homes, eating at their tables. Certainly we appreciated having places to stay, food on the table, but how we longed for a place of our own, to sleep and rise on our own schedule, even to cook our own meals. The upheaval and emotional strain wore us down and left us depressed. At the same time I felt guilty for being tired and depressed. As everyone said, we really had been extremely lucky—after all, we had our lives and the icing on the cake, *Banshee*. It could have ended so differently. At least we had a boat. We didn't have to start over completely. We would be ungrateful if we were less than elated.

Yet, in a sense we did have to start over. We had to strip *Banshee* and then begin rebuilding her. Without insurance and with limited funds, it would not be easy. Our income has always been sufficient to keep us going and take care of regular maintenance, but now we faced not only supporting ourselves, but coming up with an additional $15,000 to $20,000 to rebuild the boat.

If only the Australian government would allow us, or one of us, a work permit. Not that either of us wanted a full-time, high-powered job. We needed most of our time to work on the boat. Hiring tradesmen would be much too expensive, in addition to the fact that we do not trust others to work on our boat. Many times things are not done correctly either through indifference, incompetence or because people who have never been to sea do not realize how strong everything must be on a cruising boat. So, with so much boat work to do, neither of us wanted a full-time job— maybe just a little tutoring in the evenings to keep us in food money. But no! After speaking with numerous officials, trying to find any avenue, our attempts always ended at the same mindless *cul de sac*. We creatively suggested various things. Could we talk to yacht clubs about our experience and receive donations and sell my book? NO! Always it was no, no, no. We were tourists and therefore expected to *spend* money while here, not make it. (Actually we were going to spend bundles repairing *Banshee*.) I countered one senator's aide with whom I was speaking about the problem, "I didn't choose to come here on holiday. I was ship-wrecked! Don't you consider that an extenuating circumstance?"

The aide responded, "I might, but immigration doesn't. The government says it's not their problem, it's yours! What would your government do?"

I truly didn't know how the U. S. government would respond to a foreigner in our circumstances. I hoped with more under-standing than we were getting. What a paradox. Yachties are often viewed by authorities as bums or hippies, irresponsible people who don't want to work. But when you tell them you want to work, need to work, it's impossible.

Joy also encountered her share of bizarre and grossly unin-formed attitudes. One comment from a woman highly placed in immigration even suggested that we might be required to leave at the end of our six-month visas, rather than having them renewed. But, Joy explained, that would be in the cyclone season. The woman's response was especially callous considering we had just survived an unseasonal cyclone: "Oh, you yachties, you all use cyclones as an excuse!"

A male official Joy talked with in Canberra suggested a solution that left his complete ignorance about yachts in no doubt whatsoever. Joy told him she had teaching credentials for New Zealand which are recognized in Australia. He said, "Well, then, it's easy. Fly the boat to New Zealand or have it towed over and get a job there!"

In a strange way we had come full circle, meeting again head on with officialdom just as we had upon our arrival in Oz. At least there was now a saving grace. In between, we had met and become acquainted with many caring and concerned Aussies who would go to great extents to help us. It took this momentous disaster for us to finally meet them. We had learned one essential thing: officials and citizens may live in the same country but they function in different worlds.

All this blather and clamor about allowing an American a work permit—as it takes away a job from an Australian—becomes even more ludicrous when one discovers what is a very common practice in this country. People opt to collect the dole (which is not bad money) and then work under the table! This stratagem is so prevalent it has reached scandalous proportions in Queensland.

Sometime in August, a shipshape, 23-foot yacht tied up in the slip next to Jeff's boat where we were living until *Banshee* became habitable again. On board was a singlehander, an agile, energetic man whose well-trimmed white beard lent him the appearance of a scholar rather than an old salt. As we soon learned, Frank Anderson, a retired engineer who had designed crop dusters, had built his own boat and several others. At first Frank didn't recognize us, but when he did, he offered instantaneously to help us work on *Banshee*. For the better part of two weeks, Frank became a regular, often ready and waiting for us to start in the morning.

In addition to his multiple skills and boundless energy to tackle any task no matter how small or laborious, Frank injected a contagious enthusiasm through his ever present quick wit. Immediately he perceived that our spirits were at a low ebb.

Instead of ignoring our emotions, he spoke about them sympathetically. He grasped and voiced what no one else had, that the aftermath was actually harder than the ordeal at sea because putting *Banshee* back together was a monumental task which at this stage seemed overwhelming to us. He said, encouragingly, that when it was finally completed, we would feel very good about ourselves and our experience.

Frank introduced a much needed playful element, too. Initially, at his suggestion, one day after lunch we took a bike ride before going back to work in the afternoon. Exercise, he reminded us, was essential. From then on most days saw us pedaling somewhere for half an hour or so to refresh ourselves. Our productivity actually increased. By the time we waved a temporary farewell to Frank when he left to resume his cruise north, we had *Banshee's* interior completely ready for painting and varnishing.

It was in August too, after five weeks of looking, that we finally found Peter Creese, a shipwright, who would repair the structural damage. In our half-depressed state of mind, looking for a shipwright had become a formidable task. Everyone we approached couldn't undertake the job for one reason or another. Joy was really taking this problem to heart. We did as much work as we could to prepare the boat for the shipwright by removing all the stainless steel fittings and the demolished teak toe rail. Underneath the toe rail we found the screws which had once fastened the deck to the hull were pulled loose. Some of the bolts were bent 90 degrees, indicating just how severe the stresses on the hull had been!

Of course, in the process of removing things we created more openings for water to pour inside. Probably the worst time for Joy happened one day when it rained. She was on *Banshee* and helplessly watched as the rain poured in and ran down the inside. We still hadn't located anyone to make the essential structural repairs—rejoining the hull and deck—and until they were done, we couldn't do any work ourselves and the rain would continue to come in.

August was a good month for meeting helpful people. One afternoon while Joy was working on *Banshee* by herself, a woman came over and offered her a glass of wine. Jan, soon joined by her husband, Nick, had recognized *Banshee* and came over to say hello. The Woollers, cruisers themselves, offered to help us. Nick volunteered to repair all our stainless steel for only the cost of materials and gas for welding. He carted off most of the deck stainless the following weekend and we sent more by courier to him in Brisbane.

In late June, our dear friend Joyce Irving in Auckland wrote asking if we would like to attend the Women's Book Festival being held in New Zealand from September 16 to 22. Knowing our current financial situation was very tight, she said she was trying to get our airfares sponsored. Time was flying by and attempts to arrange sponsorship were not materializing. Then, finally, late in August a message came for me to call Joyce. Success! Air New Zealand would sponsor us for half of our fares!

Elation! Joy and I were floating on air. New Zealand. We had dreamed of it so often and longed to see all our friends again. With only two weeks to get ready for departure, we had a million things to do. Number one was finishing *Banshee's* interior so we could move back aboard. Jeff Brown needed his boat back. But, there was one stumbling block. Jason was still in quarantine. After about six weeks with Stu and Wendy, animal quarantine not only allowed Jason to come to Buddina and go into quarantine on Jeff's boat with us, but they transported him at no expense to us. He couldn't go live on *Banshee* in the boatyard while in quarantine and while we were in New Zealand, he would need to stay in a cattery—also not possible while he was in quarantine. We had written a letter to the chief animal quarantine officer in Brisbane, requesting permission to land Jason. As of August 23, he would have completed nine months in quarantine, the time required.

August 23 came and went. We were getting down to the wire. A few phone calls to the man in charge brought no results. Finally we called John Biggers who had worked with us and been to see us several times. In a couple of days John phoned back. He had managed to cut through the red tape! Jason would be a free cat! John would come with the vet and they would complete all the formalities and sign the appropriate papers.

Two days before our flight to New Zealand, we took the bus to Brisbane. Jan picked us up at the airport and she and Nick hosted us until our flight left for Auckland.

It was bumpy as the plane descended through heavy cloud cover. Gradually rolling velvety green and mounds of gray rock appeared through the early morning fog. New Zealand, the land of the long white cloud, spread out below. Once again I felt myself caught up in the mystique of this majestic island country.

Joyce and Jim were there to pick us up. After exuberant hugs and kisses, we loaded our bags into their car and they whisked us to their home on Kipling Avenue. I had forgotten how beautiful it is. The trees, the sheep and cows on the hillside! I was home again. Suddenly all the cares and heartaches of the past months slipped away.

We sat around leisurely talking, catching up. After a couple of hours, Joyce began putting together a tray of hors d'oeuvres. It was at least another half hour before her secret was out. Then our friends began arriving in ones and twos, each bringing food and grog. It was a feast for our hearts as well as our palates.

Then Hilton presented us with the funds from a trust set up by Joyce. It was almost enough to pay the remaining 50 percent of our airfares! Before we left, more funds came in and took up the slack. What a wonderful gift, time with our dear friends, time to attend the book fair and a chance to promote my book. It was wonderful to be alive. While it was not the first time I had had this thought, in the midst of close friends the feeling was imbued with special warmth.

Chapter 8

Reflections

The *Saramoa* had returned to land in July without finding a trace of the liferaft dropped to *Rockin' Robin* or her four crewmembers, and the search was given up.

Two things continued to puzzle us. First, the position where we were first sighted, as plotted on the chart used by the Rockhampton Flight Service and given to us by John Ryan, seemed incorrect. Second, the search area designated on this same chart was much too far west. But until we got our possessions back from our rescuer, the *Maersk Sentosa*, which included the chart we were navigating on when the disaster occurred, we wouldn't be able to compare their chart against ours.

Originally Captain Fisher had written that he would ship our possessions to us from Taiwan. This task became too complex because of customs in Taiwan, so our possessions stayed aboard until the ship returned to Australia. That was six weeks. As soon as our bags were delivered, we eagerly got out the chart and looked. Here was our track preceding, during, and after the capsize. The position of first sighting *was* different. Our position showed us east of where the Flight Service chart put us. Even more startling, the search area shown on the Flight Service chart was up to 40 miles west of our track for the entire four days we were adrift! This information only seemed to confirm for us what we had sensed all along, that the search had been carried out in the wrong area.

In our report to Sea Safety we sent along a photocopy of our chart and the Flight Service chart, explaining what we thought had happened. We had a very interesting response from Federal Sea Safety Centre (FSSC). They sent back photocopies of their own charts showing the search area, which did not even overlap with the search area as designated on the Flight Service chart! The position they gave where we were first sighted differed from ours and, of course, from the Flight Service position. They didn't attempt to explain the discrepancies between the Flight Service charted area of search or position of sighting, but they did address the differences between their position and ours. In their explanation they reasoned that our satnav had an "error of approx (sic) 23 miles displaced to the east of your actual position." Since they fixed our position by the COSPAS/SARSAT satellite, we concluded their position was correct.

We knew our satnav was not malfunctioning, so what happened? Both of us thought back to the night we were rolled over. The winds were easterly. We checked the weather map. It confirmed easterly winds. That meant we had to drift almost due west, as the position given by Sea Safety indicated. Joy must have misplotted us. That was the only possible explanation. At that time she, naturally, was shaken and distraught. In this condition it would have been easy to make an error in plotting.

But what about the area of search? Were we outside or inside the search area? Sea Safety's charts showed us inside the search areas on Days One and Three, June 8 and June 10. (See the charts at the end of this chapter.) They based their search area on Day Two, June 9, on the incorrect assumption that we had taken a liferaft, thus the drift used was that for a liferaft. This fact explains Day Two but not the remaining two days.

Except for the second night after our dismasting—the night following our sighting—the weather improved so the winds and seas diminished. Why then did Sea Safety surmise we left *Banshee*? Perhaps their assumption was based on the wreckage they thought was from *Banshee*. We heard this supposition on the radio broadcast on Saturday evening, June 9. Still, even if the wreckage was from us, that didn't indicate the boat had gone down. Many things were torn from our decks when we rolled and many other items went when we cut the mast off.

At that time, Tim Johnston, a good friend who had been moored next to us in Buddina for five months, became well acquainted with us, our attitudes and our philosophy about seafaring. Wanting to help convey any information he thought would be helpful in conducting the search for us, he called Sea Safety and told them he knew we would only go to a raft if *Banshee* was, in fact, sinking and we had no other option. Sea Safety told

131

him they could not accept information from him because he was not official. (One wonders what "official" means.)

This same procedure occurred when ham operator Don Hopper attempted to communicate with Sea Safety, giving information about us, our boat and equipment we carry on board. The very reason Don had all this information and had spoken on the ham net with us on numerous occasions even before we entered Australia the first time, was because he was the designated liaison between the Pacific Maritime Net (run by ham operators who take daily reports on yachts at sea) and Sea Safety. He was told he was not "official" and therefore his information was of no use! Just several days after we were rescued, I called Sea Safety from Rockhampton. One of my questions to them was why they had not used Don's information. I was told, "It was not official."

Naturally we raised this question in our letter to Sea Safety. Sea Safety responded in their letter that the issue was a "storm in a teacup." Ham operators did not regard this issue as a storm in teacup. Accustomed to being involved in rescue efforts of all kinds, they were appalled by the attitude displayed by FSSC and registered their protest to Sea Safety through letters and phone calls.

Why couldn't they find us on June 8, only 15 or 16 hours after we had been sighted by two spotter planes? Sea Safety's letter states, "that you were not spotted on the 8 June is not really surprising, given the weather conditions." I can agree that anyone from an aircraft would have had difficulty detecting us, but we would have heard and seen them.

However, we have other information which I believe comes closer to explaining what happened. On a video tape shot by John Ryan at the Rockhampton Flight headquarters, we heard this story. The pilot, Captain Alister Buckingham, flew out at dawn on June 8 and located the radio beacon on the raft that had been dropped to us on June 7. When he reported that and said he did not see *Banshee,* he was told to return to the base. He disagreed with this decision. He had enough fuel to continue the search and was angry that he was ordered back. Was this a decision coming down from Sea Safety or was it issued by the Flight Centre? Sea Safety is supposed to be in control of all decisions, so one must theorize that it was Sea Safety's decision. What this, in effect, means is that the actual search for us on June 8 lasted for about two hours, probably less.

I have already explained that the pilot of the craft who spotted us on June 10 claims he was outside the search area. Sea Safety's chart shows us inside the area. I have no explanation for the discrepancy.

Perhaps most puzzling of all is why our EPIRB signal was not picked up by Sea Safety after we wired it into the ship's battery. It was picked up *after* we were rescued, but not while we were on board. When we put this question to our friend Brian Robinson, he also was curious. He was so intrigued that he called Derek Barnard and asked him if he knew why. Brian recorded his conversation with Derek and sent us a copy of the tape. Derek said he also wondered about FSSC not picking up the beacon. When he asked Sea Safety about it, he was told there were so many EPIRB signals sounding that they were confused! Somehow that answer confuses me. Sea Safety had three boats in distress, the *Rockin' Robin* and *My Affair* as well as us. Wouldn't they, as a matter of course, check out any EPIRB they heard? Very possibly there was yet another craft in distress.

Federal Sea Safety organized the search that led to our rescue. This effort involved literally hundreds of persons including the administrative staff at Sea Safety, ground crews, civilian volunteers as well as Australian Army, Navy and Air Force personnel who flew the aircraft and those who went along as observers. To these people we owe a debt for our very lives.

Joy and I were found. Then why are we raising these questions? We have no desire to antagonize or alienate anyone, least of all those who rescued us. Our concern is that four men were lost, perhaps needlessly so, and there will be others in distress in the future. Shouldn't those in charge of search-and-rescue want to review everything that happened in an effort to pinpoint problems and identify areas that can be improved? If honest appraisal is part of it, why were we not invited to an evening when Sea Safety and other authorities involved in the search spoke at the Royal Queensland Yacht Squadron (RQYS) in Brisbane about the search for *Rockin' Robin* and *Banshee*? At that time or any other time, we would have been happy to discuss the search and rescue with them, and we had stated this. Yet there has been no attempt to talk with us. A true dialogue could, in fact, have been very beneficial, but as Australians have seen with the *Rockin' Robin* case, Sea Safety has been less than candid and has assumed a defensive posture regarding any questions which might indicate they have made mistakes. To be sure, there has been no attempt to have a dialogue with us or to give satisfactory answers to some legitimate questions we have raised.

When we spoke at the Queensland Multihull Association at the Caledonian Club in Brisbane, one of the members inquired why we were not present at the RQYS meeting. We replied that we had known nothing about the meeting. He then informed us that the military had been very concerned that we had not boarded the liferaft they dropped to us. If that is their concept of how we should have handled the situation, then indeed they need to hear our response. The four men on the *Rocking Robin* were strong enough to right a ten-person liferaft in howling winds and mountainous seas, but two women, one of them seriously injured, were not strong enough to right the raft. Had the raft been upright when dropped to us we still would not have boarded it. A raft is far more difficult to spot than a yacht, far less safe than a yacht and has far less provisions than a yacht and cannot be maneuvered, while there is a good chance that a yacht can be jury rigged and sailed. In fact, there was absolutely not one positive reason why we should have abandoned ship and gone into a raft. Unfortunately, there is some question about the *Rockin' Robin* crew going into the raft dropped to them. Their yacht was still floating high in the water when they abandoned ship. It was not sinking when they left her. The bottom line is, the men who got into the raft died. We survived because we did not get into the raft.

I believe it is almost impossible for someone who has not been through the harrowing experience of sustaining severe damage in horrendous weather to know the kinds of emotions survivors may experience when help appears on the scene. One of the greatest pitfalls may be that survivors are vulnerable and they *expect* their rescuers to know more about the business of rescue than they do themselves. Therefore, when a raft is dropped to you, you feel a strong compulsion to get into it! I remember our own puzzlement when they dropped the raft to us. I know that usually one cannot be picked up off the deck of a sailboat by helicopter because the prop may tangle with the mast. Generally rescuers want the crew either to jump into a raft so they can be plucked from it or to swim free of the boat. These thoughts went through my mind as the raft landed beside us upside down in the water. Yet it was almost dark and there was no helicopter standing by, so I questioned why the raft had been dropped.

Despite the claims made for liferafts and their seaworthiness, I remain dubious about them in extreme conditions. I am dubious about liferafts for yet another reason. On many occasions we have been told that it is almost physically impossible for women to pull themselves into a liferaft. It requires enormous upper body strength, more than most women have. A second problem is that breasts also seem to hinder women's ability to board liferafts. Barbara Oldfield, a former police inspector from Melbourne, told me that her yacht club decided to purchase liferafts which could be used by club members for long distance races. Barbara was part of the committee who tested various kinds of rafts to determine which type to purchase. In a swimming pool, several women, including Barbara who was in tiptop physical condition, could not board any of the rafts save one and this one only with great difficulty. Remember the test was conducted in a swimming pool, not in a storm tossed sea!

Rafts are difficult for males to board also. As soon as you step on the ladder extending down into the water, the tendency is for the raft to tip forward and overturn. Compound these difficulties with monstrous, breaking seas and you begin to comprehend some of the difficulty of boarding a raft in storm conditions.

Experienced cruisers know all the minuses about liferafts. Most of us remember the Fastnet Race tragedy of 1979. Out of 303 yachts that crossed the starting line, 23 boats were abandoned when bad weather disabled them. As a result of abandoning ship, 15 people died. As I recall, all but one or two of the vessels survived the storm and were found and towed in. The lesson learned here, at the expense of considerable loss of life, was that those remaining with their boats survived, those abandoning did not.

Naturally Joy and I followed all the events connected with *Rockin' Robin* with tremendous interest.

Was the search for *Rockin' Robin* called off prematurely? Officially it ended Sunday evening, June 10, and was only resumed the following day at the request of Mrs. Wiltshire, the skipper's spouse. The resulting delay meant that the plane only arrived on station at 12:11 p.m. rather than at first light, again a lapse that might have been critical. The search lasted from June 8 until June 11. Was that exhaustive? Many people have survived much longer than four days in a liferaft. The record is 119 days by a man and woman, the Baileys. So, surely, the elapsed period of time should not have been the decisive reason for discontinuing the search.

When the men were last sighted, the wind had moderated to 40 knots. If the men did survive Friday night, the 16-hour gap might well have been critical to their being found. It took five hours for the Orion 251 to locate the empty liferaft, but then it only searched for another two and a half hours for the second raft. All in all one would have to conclude that the problems fall into two basic areas: poor communication between Sea Safety and the groups actually involved in carrying out the search, and poor coverage and follow up in searching primarily because there was neither any means of communicating with the men in the raft nor any means of locating the raft.

A year after the loss of *Rockin' Robin,* the June 11, 1991 issue of *The Bulletin with Newsweek* published an account of the search for the raft together with a criticism of equipment and methods. Perhaps no one is better qualified than its author, Laurence Gruzman, who is Queen's Council and who, as a member of the volunteer civil service search-and-rescue unit (SAR), spent over 100 hours flying in the search for the lost *Rockin' Robin* raft. Gruzman, himself a yachtsman, was once overturned while sailing from Sydney to Lord Howe island in conditions like those that beset *Rockin' Robin.*

As Gruzman indicates, a number of problems and responses led to the loss of the four crew. By radio the crew reported that they were no longer able to control the incoming water aboard their vessel. Gruzman suggests that a power-driven pump with hoses and fuel would probably have saved the vessel and crew. Routinely the U.S. Coast Guard makes such drops successfully. Unfortunately, no organization except SAR in Australia could drop a pump and they could not get to the stricken vessel.

In 1985 the volunteer SAR unit based in New South Wales imported a U.S. Coast Guard pump, but neither Sea Safety nor the Civil Aviation Authority (CAA) was interested in using such equipment as they reasoned their job was not to save boats from sinking.

Since the rescuers had no facilities to drop a pump, their approach was to let the boat sink and drop a raft to the crew. The Royal Australian Air Force (RAAF) dropped two large rafts and two supply containers attached to the rafts by 393 yards of waxed rope. These were identical to the ones dropped to us. This antiquated system, developed in Britain in 1942 for saving seamen and air crew, proved to be disastrous for the *Rockin' Robin* crew.

The raft units were intended to be dropped to windward of the stricken yacht so as to drift down to them. This did not happen, so the crew actually managed to sail their yacht with torn sails to the nearest raft. It is unlikely that the crew understood that the containers held food and water, as they made no effort to retrieve the supplies. Nor would this task have been easy, given the prevailing high winds and seas and the type of line attached to the containers. It was 6mm line (only fractionally larger than 3/16s of an inch) which breaks in rough conditions and would cut through flesh when pulled on.

The raft the men boarded had no supplies on board. No food, no water, no EPIRB. This must have come as a big surprise to the men because commercial rafts are always outfitted with water, food, fishing lines, first aid supplies and signalling devices.

The rafts used by RAAF and CAA are not tested for dropping from aircraft and therefore have a 50% chance of landing upright on the water. In this case the raft landed upright but by the time the men got to it, it had turned upside down. It took heroic effort to right it.

Shortly after they boarded the raft, it capsized again, throwing them back into the water. After a struggle they managed to right the craft. In an effort to make it more stable, one man lay on top of the canopy while the other crew partially deflated the upper chamber of the raft. These actions, together with deployment of a small sea anchor, seemed to render the raft more stable.

The crew boarded the raft around 8 a.m. and with an RAAF Orion circling overhead they no doubt felt confident that their situation would soon be ended. They had been informed that a French warship would arrive in about 20 hours, but in the night they were lost and never seen again.

What went wrong? At first the crew thought their yacht would sink at 3 a.m., but it was still afloat at 10 a.m. and no one saw it sink. The yacht should have carried a liferaft. Instead they had only a Zodiac inflatable and its single air chamber had deflated. If the *Rockin' Robin* had had a proper liferaft aboard supplied with emergency items, the men would have been better off. As it happened they ended up being totally dependent upon being found and rescued.

Gruzman rightly criticizes the RAAF for dropping a raft without a radio, an EPIRB, food, water and signalling devices on board. Secondly, the search area was 621 miles from Australia but only 372 miles from Noumea. Australian aircraft could have been flown to Noumea and a search mounted from that base.

What has been done: personnel and administrative changes have made the new Australian Maritime Safety Authority more effective than Sea Safety. The new organization has ordered some U.S. Coast Guard pumps and precision aerial delivery systems (PADS) equipment. The CAA has made limited improvements, but it still has 250 liferafts without supplies or EPIRBs. RAAF still has about 50 rafts. The official report says the *Rockin' Robin* raft capsized three times and the empty raft was continually spinning and capsizing in the rough seas and wind.

The scenario Gruzman sets for the *Rockin' Robin* crew is that they managed to survive in the raft only gradually realizing that the searchers had lost them and they were adrift in a raft with no supplies and no way to catch water. Gradually they began to die.

Another scenario is equally plausible. The *Rockin' Robin* crew probably lost their lives when the raft capsized. The official report states that the raft capsized three times while observers were watching. Very possibly the men were too tired and too cold to right the raft when it capsized again and life ended more quickly by drowning or hypothermia.

The bottom line is that these four deaths could probably have been prevented. It was not wise to encourage these men to leave their yacht. If only the crew had the means to keep it afloat, they might have not died.

This is a treacherous coast with a lot of commercial shipping, a very large fishing fleet and a considerable number of pleasure craft. It is not uncommon to have vessels in distress. The authorities are certainly well aware of the horrendous conditions they must face in search and rescue on this coast. One of the most important things they could do is educate boaters to stay with their craft, only taking to a liferaft when the boat is actually going down.

On the following pages are two charts showing the area of our dismasting and rescue. The first chart on page 140 gives the official search areas as reported to us by Federal Sea Safety Centre in Canberra.

The second chart on page 141 shows our track from June 5 through June 10 when the *Maersk Sentosa* picked us up around noon. The designated search areas are taken from the chart given to us by John Ryan. He obtained it from the Rockhampton Flight Service officers.

It will be seen by comparing this chart with the chart from Federal Sea Safety Centre what an enormous difference there is in the search areas indicated by the two groups.

Note: the date on these charts is given by month and day. Time is in four digits based on 24 hours.

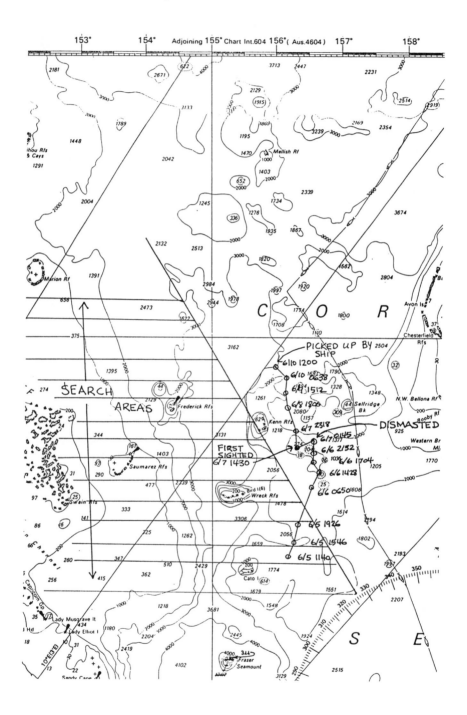

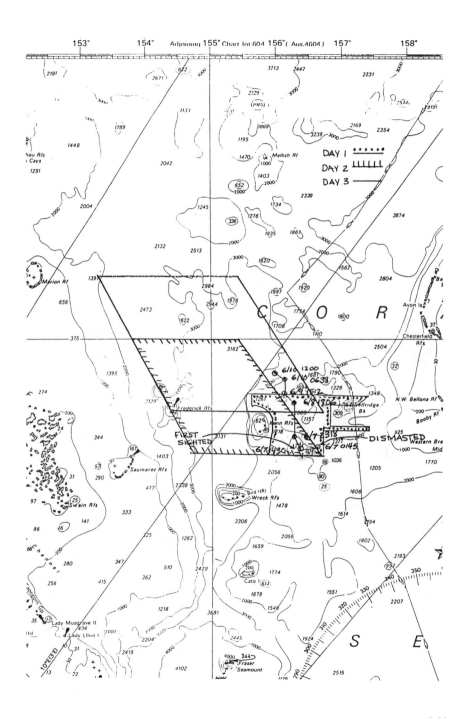

Chapter 9

In Retrospect

Naturally after our disaster we asked ourselves many questions. What could we have done differently? Could we have prevented the dismasting had we taken another course of action?

The strategy we adopted resulted from our consideration of many factors, one of these being that we and the weather forecasters thought the low would follow the coast of Australia, generally going south. Unfortunately it didn't. Instead it veered east and came directly over us. (See the weather maps at the end of this chapter.) This development was a surprise, but in retrospect it probably should not have surprised anyone. The 1035 millibar high south of us was pushing up against the low, blocking its progress south. The low followed the line of least resistance and flowed eastward.

What this meant for us was not only that we took the full brunt of the cyclone, but we ended up in the worst part of the semicircle where the winds are the most severe. In the southeastern sector, we received hurricane force winds from the low itself, in addition to the speed at which the system was moving. In this case it traveled between 15 to 20 knots, which explains why we got winds as high as 100 knots. Had we known the cyclone would take this track, we would have sailed south.

There is another reason why we probably would have fared better had we gone south as opposed to north. When the storm hit us, we were over a seamount where depths were sometimes as shallow as nine fathoms. These shallow waters developed very nasty and irregular seas. We can only approximate our position when we were rolled, in a depth of only about 40 fathoms. But it could have been as shallow as 9 fathoms (54 feet)! That became apparent when we later studied the chart. Had we been in deeper water, the seas would have been more regular and therefore less treacherous.

It's instructive to consider where *Pom Pom* was—a Herreschoff 28 and the smallest craft in the cyclone—and of all the boats in this storm, she was only one undamaged. They were hove to under bare poles in depths from 820 to 1093 fathoms. While they had breaking seas and massive waves, Barry said they did not experience the steep, irregular seas that we saw. In *Heavy Weather Sailing,* Adlard Coles points out that gusts or winds of hurricane force create chaotic seas. Other influences are current, shoals and other obstructions on the bottom. What makes waves dangerous is not size as much as shape and steepness. It is critical in ocean storms, the book advises, to remain in deep water.

Would we have fared better hove to under bare poles rather than sailing on a close reach under storm jib? We will never know, but Joy believes it would have prevented us from rolling. Positioned as we were just 30 miles or so east of Kenn Reefs, heaving to could very likely have resulted in our being pushed onto the reefs. I disagree with Joy. I believe that being hove to in the seas we experienced would have been very dangerous. *Heavy Weather Sailing* mentions that the element of risk in lying ahull is of being knocked down by freak waves or of being rolled over 360 degrees.

We also have to address the question of why the mast collapsed. Capsizing does not always result in dismasting. Obviously in our case, the weak link was our mast which crumpled from within in two places, a compression failure. All the stays, shrouds and turnbuckles were undamaged. We were using running backs of very light wire, which led to a four-part block and tackle attached to a padeye on the deck and tensioned by hand. According to Andy Wall, a friend who is a professional rigger, this arrangement may have allowed a springiness on the runner, allowing the mast to pump. A better arrangement would be to have the runner led directly to a block on the deck and onto a windward winch. In rerigging we will make the running backs of 5/16 inch wire with a rope tail so they can be pulled in around a winch.

We have concluded that the mast primarily failed because of metal fatigue. Secondarily, perhaps, was because the mast section was undersized. It was only a 5 inch by 6 3/4 inch section. (The new section will be 5 1/2 inches by 8 inches). Unquestionably the biggest factor in mast failure was metal fatigue. For 20 years this mast has endured the stress and strain of heavy cruising (70,000 miles with Joy—across the Pacific three times—plus whatever mileage under the first owner, designer Halsey Herreschoff who raced her in the SORC). It went down years ago and was repaired with a sleeve. This time the failure was directly below the reinforced sleeve and several feet below the spreaders. Over the years the mast has had various fittings added and removed, which ultimately weakens it. Most people we have talked with never think about the fact that aluminum masts weaken and therefore have a limited life. Sailors are more likely to focus their attention on the wire stays and shrouds. Still, we have met a surprising number of people who think stays will last a lifetime! In our opinion, stainless steel wire with roller swages is good for a maximum of eight years and I personally wouldn't feel comfortable trusting it that long on a cruising boat. We changed our eight-year-old rigging in New Zealand and found three cracks in the upper roller swages!

Another important consideration is how we personally responded to the situation. I've always heard that no one ever really knows how she or he will respond in an emergency. I believe that is true. In other emergencies I have managed to keep my cool and be able to think clearly. In this predicament I suffered a lot from shock. I'm most thankful we didn't have an immediate crisis that sank the boat within 30 seconds or three to four minutes. Perhaps I would have responded instinctively, doing the right things. I don't know. What I do know is that both of us were totally surprised by the effect of shock when, even three hours after the dismasting, we both experienced a type of paralyzing shock when attempting to go on deck to cut loose the mast. Whenever I have thought about a situation requiring me to abandon ship, I never once gave any thought to shock and how it might affect me or Joy.

Because shock can render one sluggish in thought and action, this is the best argument I can think of to recommend that anyone going to sea should contemplate all types of emergencies and how she or he would handle them. What actions would you take, what kinds of supplies would you need? I believe it is instructive to put yourself through this exercise. Probably the more sailing we do the more necessary it is to think about it actively, because we all tend to become complacent about things we do all the time.

In some ways I feel we could have been better prepared. We should have had at the ready a ditch bag containing clothing, nonperishable food, fishing gear, flashlight and extra batteries and a knife. We have some of these items in the raft, but more would be useful if the raft had to be used. After careful consideration, we have listed what we would like in a ditch bag for our future cruising. You will find the list of items at the end of this book.

Bob Bedford pointed out to me the importance of having a hydrostatic release for a liferaft. This device, working on pressure, is preset so the raft inflates when the water reaches a certain depth. A hydrostatic release would be especially useful if the vessel sinks quickly because without the automatic release, the liferaft could easily sink with the boat.

Our EPIRB was conveniently placed for taking with us into a liferaft and our flares were also together in a plastic container. I now know I will always carry extra batteries for an EPIRB. I have given serious thought to having a manually operated desalinizer in the ditch bag or packed in the raft. Short of that, the next best thing would be some means of giving yourself a salt water enema; a length of surgical rubber tubing would be fine. The primary reason the Baileys were able to survive 119 days in a raft was because, being a nurse, she realized they could prevent dehydration by taking salt water enemas. Because the bowel is a semipermeable membrane, it does not allow salt to pass, but it does absorb water. Many people expect if they had to go to a raft they would survive by eating fish. What they often do not realize is that the body needs a substantial amount of liquid to process protein.

Until this disaster I had never shot off a flare! I believe everyone should know what to expect of the flares they carry. For offshore cruising the most effective flares are those for a Very Pistol, which incidentally is illegal in Australia without a license, and hand-held parachute flares. The tiny smoke flares sold in marine stores are totally ineffectual in heavy winds as the smoke dissipates too quickly to provide a marker. It would be useful to shoot off some flares to see how effective various types are. Also, program yourself to point the flare downwind. If in a panic, one forgot and pointed it upwind, it would be disastrous.

Everyone should know how long their EPIRB will operate. Also from now on we want one we can service ourselves. It should be checked frequently, but do so only at the designated time or it will be picked up as a distress signal! We only relied on the manufacturer's date and never checked our EPIRB. We were lucky it worked when we needed it.

It is important to limit or minimize damage by fastening everything down. All hatch boards inside the boat should be secured so they will not fly out in a knockdown or capsize. There must be a way of fastening the main hatch from inside to prevent seas from washing it out. Stoves must be secured so they can't come loose if the boat turns over. (We know any number of people whose stoves are not secured.) Boats with glasses and mirrors should take precautions that these cannot fly around or be struck by other objects in rough weather.

All the ship's batteries must be securely tied down. Ours were secured with stainless wire tightened by a turnbuckle. Even so, the engine-starting battery partially tipped over but not enough to dump its acid. Some cruisers actually carry an extra supply of battery acid. Fuel tanks must be secured so they don't get loose and become battering rams.

All outside lazerettes and lockers must be locked when at sea.

If using the backstay as an antenna for the HF radio, it is a good idea to have whip antennas for emergency use. We had whip antennas, but the radio failed to work after taking water in the capsize.

It makes good sense to try to position the electronics in the driest part of the boat, but in the case of a roll, every place is likely to get wet. Covers to protect the radio and other electronics from water damage would be good. Thanks to *Banshee's* deep bilge we had no water above the cabin sole right after we rolled. In boats with a shallow bilge, this is indeed a major problem; even without a knockdown or capsize, such a boat is frequently wet below and lets water into the lockers.

Indispensable to us during our ordeal was the manual bilge pump mounted inside the boat under the cabin sole. This is one safety feature I would not want to be without. We have a second manual bilge pump mounted at the stern and operable from the helm. When we left *Banshee,* the inside bilge pump was working. When the boat came back, we noticed that the pump was broken. At first we thought George in his haste to pump out the boat might have forced it too far and broken it. However, when we removed it, we could see the stainless bolt attaching the plastic mount to the diaphragm had rusted, in the process exploding the surrounding plastic! The pump, a Whale Titan, was about five years old and had rarely been used. Furthermore, even though mounted in the bilge, because of its location just under the cabin sole, it was never submerged until the week when we left the boat. We were very surprised to see the stainless bolt had rusted through and wondered if it was inferior quality stainless.

Because the radar dome was mounted on its own mast, along with a whip antenna, we did not lose either item. Likewise the satnav antenna was attached to an awning gallows on the stern rather than to the mast. It too survived and worked throughout our ordeal.

One still hears a lot of discussion and argument as to which mast is best on a cruising boat: deck-stepped or keel-stepped. Keel-stepped masts win hands down because they break above the deck, leaving a stump which can then be used to jury rig. The deck-stepped mast will likely end up as a battering ram which could very quickly hole the vessel. Another advantage of a keel-stepped mast is that it is unlikely to tear away part of the deck, whereas a deck-stepped mast might. In very heavy seas this damage would make the boat unseaworthy and be very difficult to repair at sea in storm conditions.

One of the problems we would have faced had we jury rigged was the lack of attachment points on the mast stump for fastening stays. We would have tried attaching them to the boom we intended to use as an extension for the mast. But attachment places on the boom were very limited. Since our disaster, it occurred to us that having mast steps would be a good idea, both to facilitate getting up the mast stump and for attachment points for rigging. We have added them to our new mast.

For the first time we have begun to question having opening ports. They provide excellent ventilation, especially in the tropics, but the disadvantage is that they are vulnerable in heavy weather. Perhaps the best way to deal with them is to have wood or plexiglass shutters that can be fitted over them when making a passage. In the tremendously heavy seas that were battering us, water showered in and I was worried something would bash one in. Both *My Affair* and *Winnifred* had their ports knocked out in this storm. Above all, one should never go to sea in a boat with large glass windows.

The type of liferaft one carries is an important issue. I used to think a Tinker, which is a raft capable of being rowed or sailed, was a good idea. After seeing those seas we were in, I have definitely revised my idea. Because of its dinghy shape, I know it would not have survived the seas we saw. Even the traditionally shaped square, round or octagonal, canopied liferaft would have been very likely to turn over. And, as we know, *Rockin' Robin's* raft and the one deployed to us did overturn. Liferafts, as the Fastnet disaster should have taught all of us, are a last resort. If your boat is floating, stay aboard, stay with her as long as possible, even if it means frequent or steady pumping. Pump. If in the end you have to abandon ship, at least you may have bought some time and conditions may have calmed. Go to a raft only if you have no other option.

A trawler boat captain Joy spoke with recently did not have very encouraging words about liferafts. He related some terrible accounts of mates who had been in rafts. In heavy seas, rafts commonly spin down the crests causing some survivors to become very sick. Some of them opt to jump out to their deaths rather than stay in the gyrating raft.

Why have a liferaft? There are many conditions or situations in which a raft is the only recourse and they have saved lives. What I think people must grasp is that in a survival storm boarding a raft is very difficult and the probability of the raft remaining upright is slim. Far better insurance might be trying to make the boat itself unsinkable. When I talked with the commodore of the Queensland Multihull Yacht Club, he related that multihull owners today are not bothering with liferafts; they try to build their craft so that they are unsinkable. This concept of the "mother ship" as the liferaft was recently shown to work. The most remarkable example of this idea is the New Zealand boat, *Rose-Noelle*, a trimaran whose four crew survived in the upside down craft for 119 days until finally washed ashore on Great Barrier Island.

Clearly, disaster at sea is a subject no one wishes to dwell upon. Each of us thinks, "It will never happen to me." Even though unpleasant, the subject bears considerable thought. Never again will I dismiss it so lightly, and I think cruisers who know us took more notice about their own safety preparations after our mishap, one very positive outcome of our experience. It shook others out of their lethargy.

Yet another type of "lethargy" concerns me. Common sense dictates that everyone who goes to sea in small craft should be able to handle the boat and navigate. But in practice this often is not the case. Most of the cruisers we see are a twosome, a man and a woman. All too often the women either don't know how to handle the boat or it is not rigged so they can physically do it. Many women have not even learned to navigate or to plot a satnav fix. I don't believe all these women are suicidal or have a hidden death wish, but they are playing Russian roulette. This situation can only prevail when these women and their male companions do not think about what the consequences are if the man has a serious problem such as a heart attack or falls overboard. It's easier to believe "It will never happen to me." Unfortunately, it does not even have to be a terrible disaster. It might only be that the man has broken an arm or a leg and cannot function. But it can soon turn into an unnecessary disaster if the second person, the woman, is unprepared to deal with routine and emergency situations herself.

Having become more conscious of the necessity to be prepared in an emergency, I have recently begun to read any literature I can find on survival at sea. I soon discovered something very disturbing. It appears that official publications—those produced by government agencies intended for use by commercial shipping—often give poor or even erroneous instructions for those who have to abandon ship and go to a liferaft.

149

As we all know, the greatest threat a survivor faces is dehydration with death following very quickly. At most only a few days supply of fresh water is contained in liferafts. In some instances survivors may be lucky enough to have brought a few gallons of fresh water in jerry jugs from their sinking craft, probably though, not more than about five gallons. More often it seems, those abandoning ship have at most a week's supply of fresh water.

When addressing this problem, two official publications, one British and one Australian, state unequivocally that the survivor must not ever drink sea water. The British Board of Trade Shipping Notice No. M.500 Drinking of Sea Water by Castaways says:

Seafarers are reminded that if cast away they should NEVER UNDER ANY CIRCUMSTANCES DRINK SEA WATER which has not been through a distillation plant, or de-salinated by chemical means.

A belief has arisen recently that it is possible to replace or supplement fresh water rations by drinking sea water in small amounts. This belief is wrong and DANGEROUS.

Drinking untreated sea water does a thirsty man no good at all. It will lead to increased dehydration and thirst and may kill him.

Even if there is no fresh water at all it should be remembered that men have lived for many days with nothing to drink, and therefore the temptation to drink untreated sea water must be strongly resisted.

If anything the position stated in the Australian government's Survival at Sea Instruction Manual published by the Department of Transport and Construction is even stronger.

Drinking sea water will greatly reduce the chances of survival. The salt put into the body requires more water to dissolve it for the kidneys to pass it out. This water can only be taken from the body cells, hence increasing dehydration and increasing thirst. Thus a vicious circle is set up, and the more sea water drunk, the greater the thirst. Continued drinking of sea water is fatal.

Persons attempting to drink sea water must be physically restrained for their own good. War-time experience indicates that the death rate in survival craft where salt water was drunk was 7 to 8 times higher than in craft where no sea water was drunk

The date of the British Shipping Notice is 1975 and that of the Australian manual 1964. These dates are significant because in 1952, the French physician Alain Bombard, after having spent considerable time researching this very problem, began the second part of his study, using himself as a guinea pig. (The account of his survival appears in his book, *The Bombard Story*, translated by Brian Connell.) Bombard set himself adrift with only a few cans of fresh water and a supply of fishing gear, both sealed. Neither of these containers was ever opened. In an inflatable raft, Bombard pursued a four-stage journey to carry out his experiment. His first leg took him from Monaco in the Mediterranean to Tangiers. From Tangiers he carried on to Casablanca, then to the Canary Islands. The final stage of his experiment, the longest and most strenuous, lasted from October 19, when he left the Canary Islands, to December 23, when he landed in Barbados. These 65 days, during which Bombard drank sea water when he had no fresh and managed to feed himself from fish caught on improvised fishing gear, should have changed the traditional view that raft survivors must never drink sea water or eat fish. Yet, obviously, it has not.

Bombard proved that the human body can survive by drinking sea water. He has spelled out exactly what one must do in order to survive. He calculated that the human body can handle 800 milliliters (a little less than a quart) per day if drunk in two or three mouthfulls every three hours for eight to ten hours. (I would question if this amount should be reduced for a smaller person.) This procedure can be followed for six or seven days, but then one must drink fresh water for at least one day before resuming the intake of sea water. From time to time, Bombard was able to collect rainwater, dew or hypotonic liquids—any liquid whose composition is similar to that of fresh water because it does not contain large quantities of dissolved salts. The main sources of hypotonic water at sea are fish juice, contained along the spine, and in the blood of sea turtles.

On the first leg, Bombard had a companion, though for the rest of his experiment he was alone. Upon leaving Monaco for the first four days, Bombard drank sea water while his companion did not begin drinking it until the second day. During this time, both men had normal urine and no sensation of thirst. As Bombard stresses, it is essential to begin drinking sea water before you become dehydrated.

They found a good remedy for the feeling of thirst was to cover their faces with a cloth soaked in sea water. After the initial four/three days on sea water, they had two days on sea perch which provided them with food and liquid. There followed six more days of sea water, then two days of fish—without any internal complications.

For some reason many authorities do not accept Bombard's claim that by strictly following his guidelines humans can safely drink sea water for a limited period. Fortunately we have more examples of people who have survived by drinking limited amounts of sea water or by stretching their water supply by mixing fresh water with sea water.

In 1947, Thor Heyerdahl added 30-40 percent sea water to fresh water. In addition to Heyerdahl, many others have used sea water to supplement fresh water, fish liquid and turtle blood.

An excellent book thoroughly covering all aspects of raft survival is *Survival at Sea* by Bernard Robin. It has been translated into English by Richard Simpkin and it was published by Stanley Paul in 1981.

As Robin indicates, Bombard's experience and that of other survivors provides us with several options. We could choose to begin the sea water regimen in the hours immediately following shipwreck; we could drink our fresh water in large enough quantities so as to begin drinking sea water before becoming excessively dehydrated; we could drink fresh water one day, salt water the second or combine fresh and salt water. Whichever plan one chooses would depend on the person's particular circumstances, but ultimately any of these methods would be beneficial by buying more time in which to begin catching seafood and rainwater and time to be found and rescued.

The entire question of drinking sea water can be eliminated if one has a watermaker. I have seen several models offered. One, the Survivor 06, costing about $500, weighs less than 3 pints of canned water. It produces 2 pints of fresh water an hour or up to 6 gallons per day. Manually operated, it functions by using a high quality reverse-osmosis membrane which purifies the water and removes viruses and bacteria. Constructed of glass reinforced thermoplastic, it will not corrode and is guaranteed for one year.

A more expensive manually operated model, the Survivor 35, costing about $1300, produces 1.4 gallons of water per hour. Weighing less than seven pounds and being only 22 inches long, it is small enough to be included in an abandon ship bag.

I recommend anyone making offshore passages read Robin's book as it contains the best ideas I have seen for survival in a raft. One of the best things I derived from reading Robin's book was the concept that it is possible to survive if one is willing to think about the subject seriously and make some preparations in case the worst should happen. More than that, this book left me with a very positive feeling unlike the official publications loaded down with don'ts rather than dos.

Joy and I have frequently been asked why we did not use bolt cutters to get rid of the mast. We already knew that we physically could not cut 5/16-stainless wire with bolt cutters even on land, much less on a boat that is wildly heaving and rolling in stormy seas. The size cutters that would be required would just be too unwieldy. In this situation it is not just a matter of strength, it is also a question of balance. We have also been asked why we didn't remove the cotter pins. Anyone who asks this question just has no concept of the pressure on those stays and has not seriously thought about the conditions. We were being struck by crashing seas and the rather delicate job of opening and pounding out a cotter pin was simply impossible. And finally, by sawing the stays we at least were able to save the lower Sta-Loks, a small compensation for our great loss, but a compensation nonetheless.

Repeatedly we are asked, "How can you go to sea again?" How can we not! We have been given our lives and our boat. We have not lost our love for what we were doing, nor the desire to continue on. The ocean is our world and the distant horizon still beckons. My mother summed it up well when asked by a reporter from her hometown newspaper if she wanted me to come home and give up the sea and she replied, "I want my daughter to do what she would like to do. I want her to fulfill her dreams." Joy's mother has often said to us, "It's not too often two women get to live the way they want. I'm very happy for you both." And in our visitors' book, Frank Anderson wrote, "It has been a privilege to share the friendship of two spirited ladies who have already sailed through Hell and blacked the Devil's eye." Taken together, these sentiments capture the essence of why we set sail originally and why we will do so again. You don't cease doing what you love and give up a great challenge because of one bad experience.

In looking backward I must also look to myself, where I've been, where I'm going and how I feel about everything that has happened. I believe when anyone goes through a traumatic experience and emerges from it with a new lease on life, that person will ask many questions. For me, being saved is a weighty issue. It has left me with a strong sense of responsibility to make my life count. In some strange way it is as if my life no longer belongs to myself alone but rather to the world at large, to humanity. So much energy, resources and emotions went into finding us and bringing us back, yet, we can never repay the human or monetary costs on a quid pro quo basis. I can only hope that as we go along we will be of assistance to others, that somehow we can make a difference and pass on the good that was done to us. Both of us will be eternally grateful for all the help and caring shown to us by friends and strangers alike. Henceforth, our voyages will be not only across oceans but into the depths of our humanity.

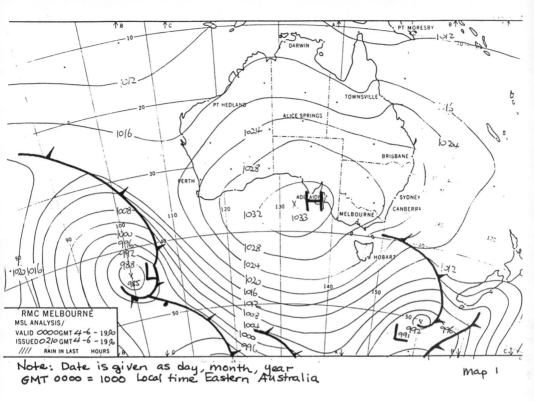

RMC MELBOURNE
MSL ANALYSIS/
VALID 0000 GMT 4-6-1990
ISSUED 0210 GMT 4-6-1990
//// RAIN IN LAST HOURS

Note: Date is given as day, month, year
GMT 0000 = 1000 Local time Eastern Australia

Map 1

Portrait of a developing storm. Notice the high near Adelaide and the low that became the cyclone between Port Moresby and Townsville.

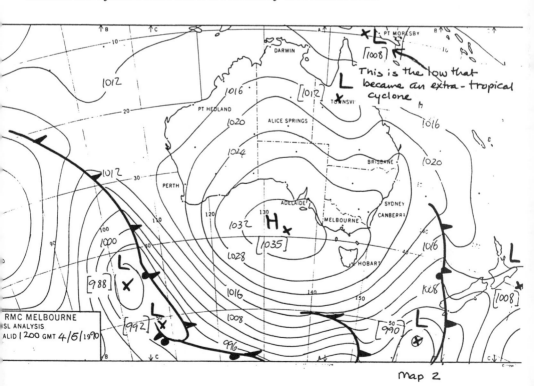

This is the low that became an extra-tropical cyclone

RMC MELBOURNE
MSL ANALYSIS
VALID 1200 GMT 4/6/1990

Map 2

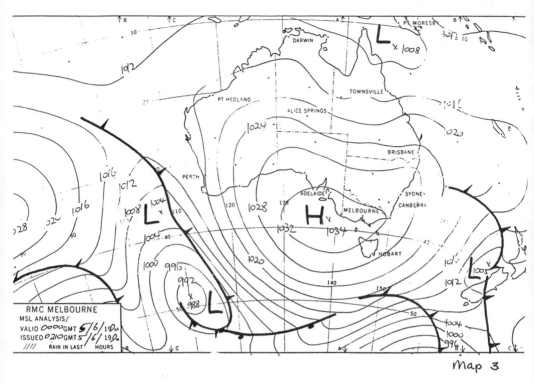

Map 3

As the high begins to move east, the low stays about the same with pressure dropping. These are the conditions that caused Joy to shreik in alarm.

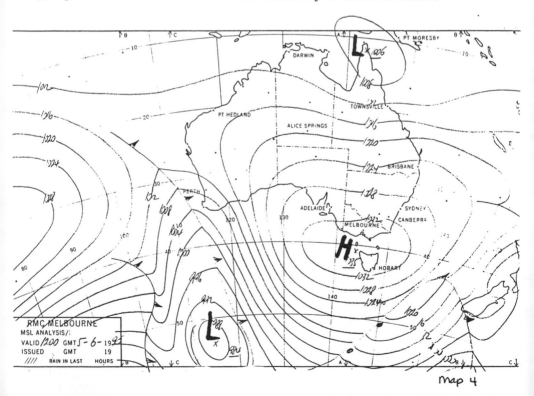

Map 4

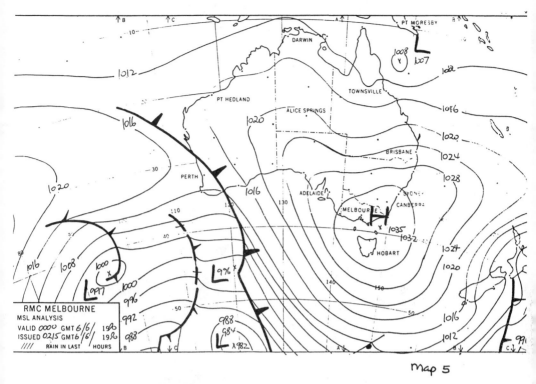

map 5

The high and the low are beginning to converge as the low moves southeast. We try to keep sailing north as the storm pounds us.

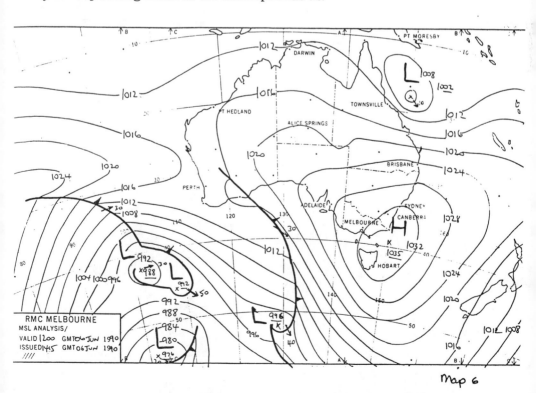

map 6

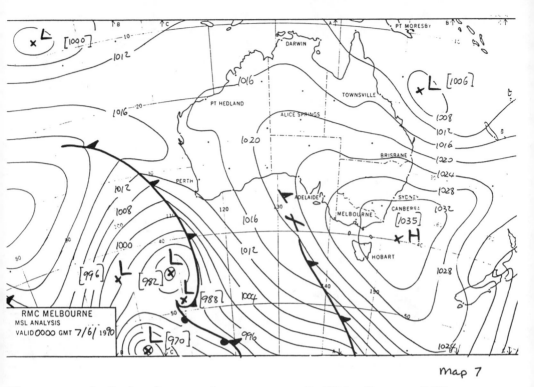

map 7

The pressure in the low drops as the storm expands. We're dismasted! When we go on deck to survey the damage, the wind is 70 to 80 knots with 40 to 50 foot waves.

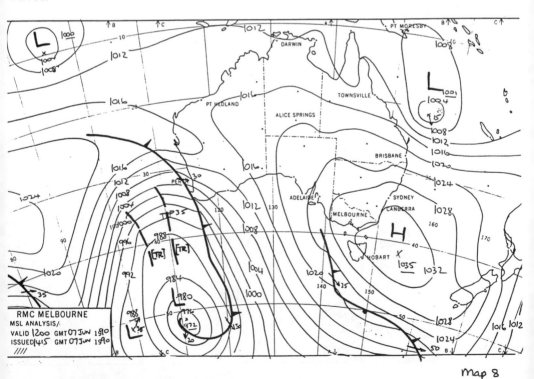

map 8

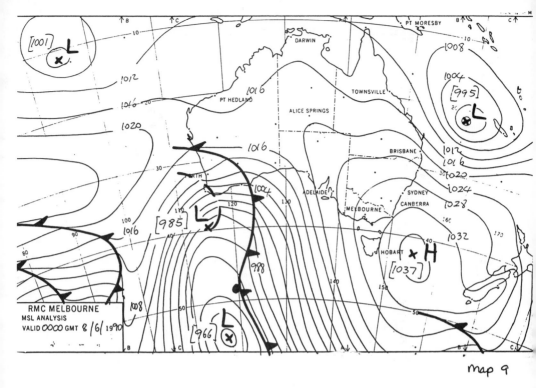

map 9

After the low came directly over us, we got hit by the other side of the cyclone. The storm center dropped to 995 and moved eastward.

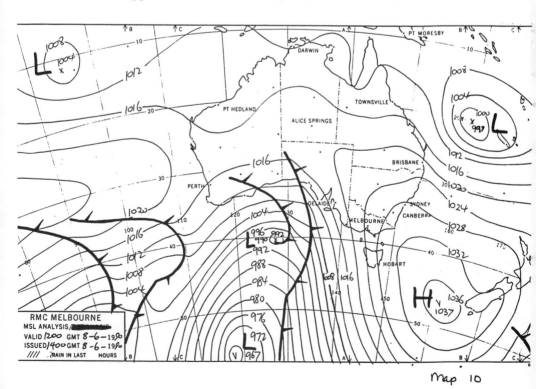

map 10

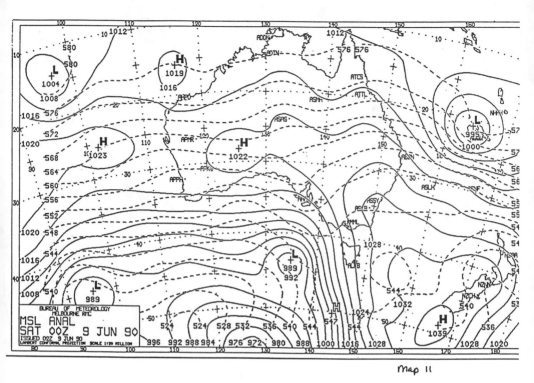

Map 11

The low moves further east as a new high develops over southern Australia.
These charts were provided by the Bureau of Meteorology's office in Queensland.

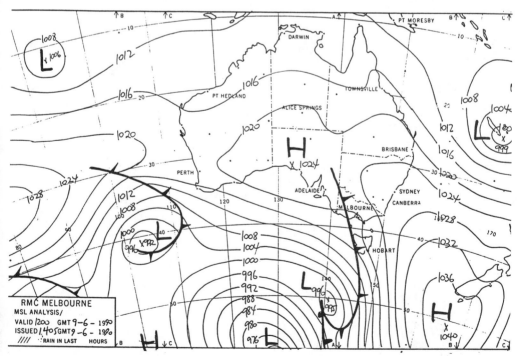

Map 12

Epilogue

A sad postscript to our story is that Bob Bedford lost the *Saramoa*. On February 1, 1991, around 6 a.m., an explosion ripped through the boat. In no time, her oil-soaked timbers blazed and burned to the waterline. This occurred in Broome, Australia where Bob and George had taken the boat to fish. Fortunately no one was aboard. Bob called us with the tragic news. The old girl, *Banshee's* savior, is gone.

But there is good news. Bob is buying another boat when the insurance company comes through.

And in early July, Brian Robinson sent us a copy of *The Mainsheet*, the Official Bulletin of the Coastal Cruising Club. At the general meeting of the club held at Sydney on June 20, Bob and George were selected to receive the Frank Nicholas Award for their salvage of *Banshee*. With this award came a plaque with their names engraved and a check for $300.

Putting Together a Ditch Bag

If all your efforts to keep the boat afloat fail and you have to go into a liferaft, having some kind of ditch bag ready to go with you is really essential. Floating ditch bags are available at a fairly steep price but with a bit of imagination and some time, it is relatively simple to make your own. Some books suggest that to give the receptacle buoyancy it can be tied between two partially filled water jugs that you will take with you when abandoning ship.

There are other methods that could work just as well. One could sew closed-cell foam into the bag, working out the amount needed to float the weight packed into the bag. Still a third possibility is to tie the container inside a partially inflated air mattress which could then be lashed securely around the ditch bag. This latter method would probably be bulkier than other solutions and for this reason might not be as satisfactory since the air mattress would have to be already inflated, ready to grab if abandoning ship quickly.

The list contains what Joy and I think are bare essentials with several additional items which might make life a little less tenuous and facilitate and hasten rescue.

EPIRB
Waterproof flashlight
Waterproof strobe light
Handheld VHF in waterproof bag
Extra batteries
Portable bilge pump
Several pieces of rope, plenty of whipping twine
Extra distress signals (ones normally carried on board)
Watermaker or solar still
Small amount of canned food, mainly carbohydrates which
    help the body to retain fluid
Can opener
Dried fruit
Condensed milk, powdered milk

Matches, waterproof or in waterproof container

One or two good multiple-blade knives

Fishing tackle—hooks, plenty of line, several large hooks which can be fixed to an oar to make a gaff; a can of mussels for bait; a plankton net can be made from pantyhose with a wire hoop

Lemon squeezer for extracting fish juice

First Aid Kit containing skin cream, sunscreen, eye lotion, antiseptics, sulfa drugs for disorders of the alimentary tract, antibiotics, suppositories against seasickness, inflatable plastic splints, rubber hose, dressings, bandages, vitamin C tablets, multiple vitamins and minerals

Stainless steel scissors

Plastic bags of different sizes

Needles and strong thread (all small items can be packed in a Tupperware container)

Underwater mask

Mirror

Whistle

Chart and plastic sextant

Paper and pencils

Air mattresses, orally inflatable, one for each person, if there is room in the raft

Several large towels or a sheet

Sunglasses and reading glasses

Foul weather gear

Extra clothes

Toothbrushes and dental floss

Even if you have a watermaker, you might also want to have emergency water containers (partially filled, enabling them to float). They will be too large to fit into the ditch bag but you can have them nearby or even lashed to the bag, ready to go into the raft with you.

If you enjoyed *Banshee's Women, Capsized in the Coral Sea*, you will want to read Jeannine Talley's first book

Women at the Helm

All her life Jeannine Talley had a dream of sailing around the world. She had her doctorate and was teaching folklore and mythology at UCLA when she bought her first boat. She started Seaworthy Women, a sailing school to teach women to sail in a supportive, non-threatening way. When she met Joy Smith, they talked about sailing around the world from their very first conversation. Joy owned a 34-foot boat and also had her own chartering business. The two became partners and decided to make the voyage. *Women at the Helm* tells how their dream became a reality and relates Jeannine and Joy's cruising experiences on their way around the world. They take turns being captain and share the magic and romance of the South Pacific. Articulate, poetic and filled with adventure, *Women at the Helm* will inspire and delight sailors and armchair sailors of both sexes and adventurous women everywhere.
(228 pages, photos, illustrations)

Ask for this book at you local bookstore or you may order it directly from—

Mother Courage Press
1667 Douglas Avenue
Racine, WI 53404

$11.95 paperback
$19.95 hardcover

Please enclude $2.00 postage and handling.